T0345625

KUNSTHAUS ZÜRICH

# The Architectural History of the Kunsthaus Zürich 1910–2020

By Benedikt Loderer

Scheidegger & Spiess

TABLE OF CONTENTS

The story of the Kunsthaus Zürich, like that of the city, is one of growth. It begins on the hill in the Künstlergütli; the Moserbau of 1910 defines the setting; the Pfister and Müller Buildings append to it; Chipperfield builds a third art museum. Here is an excursion through its architectural history from 1813 to 2020.

# The Prelude:
# The Künstlergütli

In spring 1813 the Zürcher Künstlergesellschaft (Zurich Artists' Society), itself founded in 1787, acquired a property on Halseisengasse, nowadays called Künstlergasse, for 9,200 Gulden from the 'maidens Katharina and Kleophea Ott'.[1] This purchase on credit – the commercial board of directors had to advance 9,000 Gulden – marks the first step on the winding way to the Kunsthaus Zürich that stretches out over a century. However, the residential house, situated at the time beyond the city walls and rechristened the Künstlergütli (the Little Artists' Manor), proved ill-suited for exhibitions, and the search for a new plot of land on which an art gallery could be erected for the still-modest collection soon began anew – not least because 'up on the mountain' was too out of the way for the artists. It was to no avail. The Künstlergesellschaft failed to find a building plot, and instead decided to plan on its own property. The decision, taken in 1845, was accomplished on 3 October 1847: the new building by the architect Gustav Albert Wegmann (1812–1858), christened 'Zurich's Schinkel' by architectural historian Georg Germann.

From then on, alongside the old residential house, now known as the Wirtschaft zum Künstlergütli (the Künstlergütli Inn), stood Zurich's first art museum. 'The landlord served the artists and their friends in the one house, and in the other acted as the caretaker of their works.'[2] This first Kunsthaus matched the financial standing of the Künstlergesellschaft. 'The layout in this, in terms of its dimensions and ambitions, rather modest building were remarkably simple.'[3] A stairway positioned on the narrow side of the rectangular building provided access to the two galleries, which were divided into cabinets and arranged out as an enfilade merely by means of 'coulisses'. From 1886 onwards the upper storey housed a full-length skylight gallery,[4] while the remaining rooms were lit with sidelight. When and whether gas-lighting was installed is not known, although as of 1854 Zurich had a gasworks providing for 436 public and 3,000 domestic burners.[5] The people of Zurich would have to wait until the Landesausstellung (National Exhibition) of 1883 before they could marvel at the

The Künstlergütli 'up on the mountain' was Zurich's first art museum. Left, the inn and, right the exhibition and collections building by the architect Gustav Albert Wegmann. Today the site of Karl Moser's university building.

Skylight gallery in the first Kunst haus. Using horizontal curtains the light could be dimmed. The hanging is decidedly mode above, under the roof, a runner on which cords could be vertic attached. The pictures tilt forwards, which avoids reflection

1  Vonesch 1980, p. 129.
2  Festschrift 1976, p. 5.
3  Vonesch 1980, p. 145.
4  Jehle 1982, p. 24.
5  Bärtschi 1983, p. 243.

wonders of electric light.[6] When exactly the first lights ignited in the Künstlergütli is lost in the chronicles. Nevertheless, there was an 'air-heating system from Mr Kölliker in Thalwil'.[7] In summing up, Wegmann's biographer Gian-Willi Vonesch concludes that 'with this Wegmann achieved a building unparalleled in the Zurich architecture of the times in terms of its gracefulness and elegance.'[8]

In 1847 Zurich was still in the infancy of its career as the economic capital of Switzerland. Its artists were called Heinrich Meyer, Wilhelm Huber, Jakob Ulrich; the new building was financed by a private society of artists and dilettanti from the upper classes. What emerged 'up on the mountain' was more of a clubhouse with the opportunity to exhibit than a museum. If one compares Wegmann's museum with the Musée Rath by Samuel Vaucher in Geneva, opened in 1826, or the museum on Augustinergasse in Basel by Melchior Berri, erected between 1844 and 1848, the inescapable impression is that the Zurich of the mid-nineteenth century had more affinities with 1800 than with 1900. Zurich lacked even a glimmer of the spirit pervading a museum like Schinkel's Altes Museum in Berlin of 1830, or for that matter the most influential museum building of the nineteenth century, Leo von Klenze's Alte Pinakothek in Munich of 1836. In 1847 the city had around 17,000 inhabitants, the Künstlergesellschaft barely two-dozen members.[9] Here things were still predominantly diminutive – small town, petit bourgeoisie, minor artisans. It took the railway to prod Zurich as a city from its slumber.

6  Geschichte Kt. ZH 1994, p. 165.
7  Vonesch 1980, p. 145.
8  Vonesch 1980, p. 146.
9  Festschrift 1976, pp. 6–7.

# A Makeshift Interim:
# The Künstlerhaus

Truth be told, the new building was not really satisfactory, either for the collection or for exhibitions, whereby 'in particular its deficiencies in respect of light and space were continuously felt to be onerous'.[10] For this reason exhibitions were held in the old Tonhalle (Concert Hall), situated on the Sechseläutenplatz, and after its demolition in the Alte Börse (Old Stock Exchange) at the upper end of Bahnhofstrasse. All endeavours to create a new building failed – even a museum of art and antiquities, planned together with the Antiquarischen Gesellschaft (Antiquarian Society) on the Lindenthalgut, the site of the latter-day Kunsthaus. The City Council refused to give up the parcel of land, sold to them cheaply by City Councillor Johann Heinrich Landolt in 1885 in his will, for a museum. The antiquities found a home in the Swiss National Museum on the Platzspitz in 1898, which since then has also been the Historical Museum of the Canton and City of Zurich. As it was, the Swiss National Museum, the brainchild of the Helvetic Republic's Minister for Art and Sciences, Philipp Albert Stapfer, from as early as 1799, turned out to be an additional stumbling block for a new Kunsthaus building. The original idea being to house arts and antiquities in the same institution, the long-running federal feud about which city should host the national museum effectively stymied the realisation of a Zurich art museum. It would take until 1891 for the Swiss Parliament to definitively opt for Zurich, and it was the construction of the Swiss National Museum on the Platzspitz that freed the logjam for a solo appearance.[11] Despite the opportunity, the competition for an expansion of the Künstlergütli held in 1893 ended in a fiasco. No first prize was awarded and participation was pitiful – the privilege of submitting being anyway solely reserved for members of the Künstlergesellschaft.

Still, in 1895 Zurich's first art gallery nevertheless emerged, a premises for temporary exhibitions, and this time no longer 'on the mountain' but close to the upper end of Bahnhofstrasse on the corner of Talstrasse and Börsenstrasse. Carl Kracht-Baur, the owner of the adjacent hotel Baur au Lac, donated the land to the newly founded Verein für bildende

10  Festschrift 1976, p. 5.
11  Festschrift 1976, p. 9.

Kunst Künstlerhaus (Society for Fine Art Artists' House). The architects Gustav Gull and Alfred Friedrich Bluntschli, the painter Rudolf Koller and the Neue Zürcher Zeitung editor Albert Fleiner were the leading lights of the society, which rapidly managed to boast more members than the venerable Künstlergesellschaft – in 1888 a total of 134.[12] Its membership no longer consisted of the same old-school artists and old-Zurich dilettanti, but rather was made up of businessmen, industrialists – in short the leading pillars of the new Zurich of machine engineering and commerce, who now set the pace in the newly founded art society. They hosted exhibitions for artists of all flavours and nationalities. Bluntschli supplied the design and the plans for the single-storey building. Two galleries, one with side lighting, the other with rooflight; access at ground level, the entrance adorned with an oval skylight framed by two allegorical female figures like heraldic shield-bearers.

The Künstlerhaus on the corn_ of Talstrasse and Börsenstras_ was opened in 1895. It was a low-cost building, designed b_ Alfred Friedrich Bluntschli. In_ today's jargon it would be call_ an 'art hall' or 'off space'.

12  Jehle 1982, p. 25.

The Künstlerhaus (Artists' House) looked like a huge workshop, for instance a metalworks, converted into an art gallery. There was no pretension of ostentation whatsoever, neither inwardly nor outwardly: instead there was a 'value set on the all-the-more intensive and wide-reaching effect of the artistic'.[13] Yesteryear's scene had built its own 'culture camp'.[14] With the opening of Karl Moser's building in 1914 the Künstlerhaus would disappear.

In the summer of 1896 the esteemed Zürcher Künstlergesellschaft and the new Künstlerhaus Society merged to form today's still-flourishing Zürcher Kunstgesellschaft (Zurich Art Society). From now on this body took care of both the library and the collection in the Künstlergütli up the hill and the exhibitions in the Künstlerhaus down below. Nevertheless, the consensus was that the only way to solve the ever-more-pressing lack of space had to be a new building. In 1883 a half-hearted attempt to do so on the grounds of the Künstlergütli fizzled out. In 1899 the solution seemed graspable again. The municipal authorities and the Kunstgesellschaft shook hands on a land exchange: the Künstlergütli as a swap for a plot on the Stadthausanlage (Town Hall Grounds). The result? – rejected by the voters in a referendum. Then bargaining about a development site on the Utoquai – again failure. Then the Landolt-family project, Lindenthalgut between Heimplatz and Hirschengraben, already planned in 1886, came into play again. The widow of the testator, who had a life-long right of residence in the Villa am Hirschengraben, agreed that the garden facing Heimplatz could be built on. Heimplatz first originated in 1880, being the result of extensive in-filling subsequent to the man-made abrasion of the Baroque city fortifications from 1831 onwards. At long last, after one hundred years of searching, a building site for the Zurich art museum had been found. In retrospect, and to summarise, there can hardly be a single open space around the former Schanzen (entrenchments) on which the Kunsthaus Zürich was not, at some point or another, postulated.

13  Festschrift 1976, p. 5.
14  Jahresbericht 1946, p. 5.

# 19 | The Feat:
# 10 | Karl Moser's Kunsthaus

Now, however, things began to move. In May 1903 the prize jury from the first public competition decided upon the project by the architect Haller from Zurzach, 'who then lived in Karlsruhe and in those days was probably employed in the office of Curjel & Moser'.[15] Karl Moser was a member of the jury, together with two other important architects of the time: Theodor Fischer from Stuttgart and Friedrich von Thiersch from Munich. Haller placed a ponderous corner building on the corner of the street, which itself still did not yet exist, the plan being to extend Kantonsschulstrasse right across Heimplatz and run it to Hirschengraben. The corner building connected an intermediate space with the Villa Landolt, meaning that the latter was already incorporated into the first project – an idea that Moser's annexe of 1925 would realise. Haller's layout also 'anticipated essential features of the later Moserbau'.[16] Despite this, the Kunstgesellschaft was disappointed with the outcome of the competition. The Building Commission considered none of the 57 submitted projects as worthy of realisation. The remedy? – repeat the competition. The participation criteria? – anyone who had garnered a prize in the first competition and anyone who belonged to the Kunstgesellschaft. There had been too many Germans in the first round, the locals grumbled. Moreover, these people also considered the Swiss jury member Karl Moser to be a German by virtue of his managing, together with Robert Curjel, the extremely successful architectural office Curjel & Moser in Karlsruhe between 1888 and 1915.[17]

The second competition, now underpinned by a carefully thought-out architectural programme, was decided in May 1904. This time round the prize jury was composed only of Swiss, figures faintly remembered nowadays only in the pages of architecture lexicons. No first prize was awarded, instead three second prizes were given: Karl Moser, Karlsruhe; Pfleghard & Haefeli, Zurich; Heinrich Müller and Rudolf Ludwig junior, Thalwil. The board of the Kunstgesellschaft now had to decide between the three, opting on 2 June 1904 with nine votes to two for the project by Karl Moser. The negotiations between the city

15  Jehle 1982, p. 29.
16  Jehle 1982, p. 30.
17  Rössling 1986, pp. 1 ff.

authorities, the Landolt widow, the Kunstgesellschaft and the architects made speedy progress, with the result that as little as two years later, on 15 July 1906, the referendum on the project was held. The city entrusted the land between Heimplatz and Hirschengraben to the Kunstgesellschaft and contributed 100,000 francs to the building costs.

Who precisely was Zurich building a second art museum for? The Social Democrats responded to the question with the proposal to pair the vote for the Kunsthaus with that for the Volkshaus (People's Hall). A 'yes' to the Kunsthaus had to also mean a 'yes' to the Volkshaus. The bourgeoisie, risen to status through the railways, industry and commerce that stood behind Moser's building, retorted that its explicit aim was make art open to the people. Three afternoons a week the Kunsthaus was to be open for free, and in the Annual Report for 1905 the Kunstgesellschaft explained their reasoning as follows: 'the crucial point behind the sacrifice [the free opening] was in fact the ideal notion to equally make this new Kunsthaus into a genuine Volkshaus, in the process bringing an end to the chatter about the exclusive, haughty, aristocratic character of art.'[18] The city authorities now paid 5,000 francs per year as compensation for this sacrifice.

The numerous intermediate hurdles that Moser's project overcame, from the competition to its execution, have been described in detail by Ulrike Jehle-Schulte Strathaus in her book, and can be safely skipped over here. On 17 April 1910 the Kunsthaus was ceremonially inaugurated – 99 years after the purchase of the Künstlergütli, which now had to make way for Karl Moser's other major Zurich work, the new university building. By this time the city had 191,000 inhabitants, representing eleven times the number it had been half a century earlier (whereby this equation also needs to also take account of the first municipal incorporations). The Kunstgesellschaft now had 1,064 members, whereas in 1847 it had had a mere 25.[19]

The new Kunsthaus connects two architectural volumes to form a whole: the Collections Building, a stone-built block reinforcing the future street corner, and pushed up against it a low-slung Exhibition Wing on Heimplatz – nowadays known colloquially under the labels Moser 1 and Moser 2. Collections Building is equivalent to museum,

18  Jehle 1982, p. 37.
19  Festschrift 1976, p. 5.

Exhibition Wing to Kunsthalle: from the very beginning both of them were combined in the new building. The hierarchy is clearly legible: the entrance, accentuated by a vestibule and the symmetrical 'Greek' facade, determines the principal axis and the main emphasis. The Collections Building dominates the composition. It is 'stringent and large in its elementary stereometry.'[20] The Exhibition Wing, with its double-storey wall of windows, on the other hand, has a more open, playful appearance: instead of walls with window-holes, a projecting and recessed ribbon with expansive openings, set between double columns with niche sculptures in-between.

The astonishing thing nowadays is how far Moser treated the building also as art. The sculptor Carl Burckhardt and others worked hand-in-hand with the architect, fusing the sculptural decoration with the architecture to form a unity. The situations for the large reliefs are clearly assigned by the architect, surrendering in the Collections Building to the symmetry of the facade and in the Exhibitions Wing to the tact of the window axes. The sculptor remains servant to the architect, albeit at the same time as the architect yields space for the sculptor. The wall is the medium and the background. But at no juncture is the work of the sculptor diminished to art appliqué, a later ingredient: it is always a vital, intertwined constituent element of the building. 'The attempt has been made to bring the sculpturing back into an organic correlation with the architecture and to allow it to appear as a piece of architecture', wrote Moser.[21]

Another astonishing thing is the enormous hipped roofs made of glass. They are visible from the street, and seen from Heimplatz the glazed roof becomes a temple gable. The Kunsthaus as a People's Hall? It is a treasure trove that the general populace are allowed to enter.

Whereas from the outside Moser's Kunsthaus is sober, inside 'the whole thing is bathed in Secessionist incense and choreographed with reddish Nassau marble and alternatively murmuring or opulently resplendent ornamentation'.[22] It is a stricture that a Temple of Art must give a ceremonious impression: the observation of art is a profane prayer, and this effect reinforces the sacred spirit of these rooms. This is neverthe-less contradicted by the flight of the stairway. Rather than being

The Collections Building (Mose dominates the composition of the 1910 Kunsthaus. For the th Kunsthaus Zürich the architec Karl Moser designed a stringe symmetrical stone-built box with a glazed hipped roof, with echoes of a Greek temple.

The Exhibitions Wing (Moser 2 is pushed up against the Collections Building. Its facad are more dissolved, more play They leap undulatingly back and forth. In the upper floor pa of semi-columns frame the large windows. Between them are niche sculptures.

20  von Moos 2010, p. 15.
21  Neujahrsblatt 1911, p. 44.
22  von Moos 2010, p. 13.

situated at the end of the low full-length foyer, where the axis of the symmetry would lead one to expect an ostentatious stairway, abruptly upon coming in through the main entrance one has to take a left turn in order to ascend to the upper floor. The main stairway is pressed to the side: it is a connection, not a stage, nor intended as a theatrical promenade for royalty to stride over. Up above one indeed arrives in a double-storey-height hall, but the upward progression is interrupted. The stairs stop and one crosses the hall, where after a quarter turn the stairs resume again. Contrary to what one would expect in an art museum, the foyer on the ground floor is not a lofty, ostentatious reception hall; instead one is confronted with a poorly lit 'vestibule and exhibition room', as Moser labelled it in the plans. In fact it is a wide corridor, providing access to the offices on the right and the crate-room on the left. The major axis that dominates the facade culminates modestly in the central window of the concluding wall, there where the wide stairway should cascade down into the foyer. Despite all the incense, and despite all its 'monumental Jugendstil',[23] Moser's Kunsthaus is a decidedly republican affair, a civic building. If one compares the Kunsthaus Zürich with the Palais de Rumine by the architect Gaspard André in Lausanne from 1904, the juxtaposition is not only one of École des Beaux-Arts versus Jugendstil but equally a 'princely' opulence of stairs versus republican frugality. Flaunting is not the way things are done in Zurich.

The exhibition rooms have a ceremonious appearance; the observation of art is a prof prayer. In the hall on the first floor the visitor's gaze follows the central spatial axis of the Exhibition Wing. The sculp Carl Burckhardt's Venus stand spatially dominant in the rotun

The foyer is surprisingly low a the spatial axis is devoid of a logical conclusion. Moser desig a wide, stooped corridor that at the end leads nowhere. The is no ostentatious hall with a monumental flight of stairs. Flaunting is frowned on in Zur

23 Jehle 1982, p. 90.

# An Intermezzo: Moser's Expansion Alternatives

Compared with the Künstlergütli, Moser's Kunsthaus of 1910 was gigantic. Director Wilhelm Wartmann apparently asked himself 'how the rooms could be adequately filled'.[24] Money was tight, and the idea was seized upon to rent the ground floor facing onto Heimplatz to the Bank Leu. The tenant stayed until 1976, although from 1958 onwards used only half as much space. Nevertheless, right from the start thoughts revolved around an extension. In 1919 the city bestowed the Villa Landolt to the Kunstgesellschaft, where the minor Zurich masters were housed. The remodelling was undertaken by the architect Johann Rudolf Streiff.

After the First World War Moser put his mind to how he could extend the Kunsthaus. Jehle lists six designs that emerged between July 1919 and January 1923.[25] These project sketches belong to Karl Moser's neoclassical period. Since 1915 he had served as a professor of architecture at ETH Zurich and was an adherent to Friedrich Ostendorf's demands for clear rules and new commitments. The Fluntern Church and his own residence on Krähenbühlstrasse are proof of how flexibly Moser followed the successive prevailing trends, not to mention architectural fashions. In Karlsruhe Moser had seen the remodelling of the city centre by the classicist Friedrich Weinbrenner (1766–1826) every day before his doorstep.

All of the six designs are governed by the axial symmetry of the layouts. The Collections Building becomes the centrepiece. Moser extends the symmetrical figure towards the Altstadt (Old Town) with a second Exhibitions Wing. Facing Heimplatz a palace-like row of houses is created, while the 'Greek temple' becomes the commanding focus. The six designs vary above all in how the still-vacant land behind is used and which houses on Hirschengraben are spared.

The Kunsthaus extension, a proposal by Moser in July 1919. The project is one of six alternatives. The Villa Landolt was to be demolished, the Kunsthaus extended 'backwards' with a circular building, and the Exhibition Wing symmetrically reduplicated.

24  Sondernummer 1995, p. 12.
25  Jehle 1982, p. 83.

# The Annexe:
# Moser's Extension

The collection grew. Whereas in 1910 it had contained 670 paintings and 39,000 graphic prints, fifteen years later the respective figures were 1,350 and 50,000.[26] But the Kunstgesellschaft's finances no longer allowed for the symmetrical extension Moser had planned. Any enlargement had to be economical and had to involve the Kunsthaus's own land. The only way forward was building on 'at the back', deeper into the plot. Moser placed a cube in the gap between the Kunsthaus and the Villa Landolt, which was attached to the extended Kunsthaus via a narrow intermediate building shaped like a slice of cake. Between the Villa Landolt and the Kunsthaus lay a difference in height measuring a full storey, which Moser bridged by means of this cake slice. This first extension is today known as Moser 3.

The most important room in this first extension is the reading room of the library, which in Sigfried Giedion's opinion was 'the best among the new spaces that we can present to an outsider coming to Zurich'.[27] The high reading room, lit from above, demonstrates Moser's continued evolution. Out of the mist of the 'Secessionist incense'[28] arose a disciple of Modernism, who as a professor acquainted his students with Neues Bauen. It was above all in Holland that he found his new affinities – the same 'Hollanderism' that the traditionalists of the time used as a label to vilify Modernism. The reading room was austere, a cube divided horizontally by the two white parapets of the galleries. Wilhelm Wartmann, the then Kunsthaus Director, commented thus on criticisms of the hall: 'The occasional item that has reached the ear of the proprietor is the objection that the new building is uncanny and eerie – quite simply cold, hygienic, like a hospital.'[29]

All that now remains of the 1925 extension is the facade facing the enchanted-like garden. Today the bare wall, with its five tall punched-out windows on the first upper floor, still gives a spectral trace of the sculpture gallery that was once behind it.

Longitudinal section running down the main axis of the Collections Building, Novemb 1925. The 1910 building is on the left, in the middle the anne with the reading room and libr and right the Villa Landolt. Particularly remarkable are th huge volumes of the glass roof

The reading room is the most important space in the annexe Cold and functional, for many contemporaries too austere, i bears witness to Moser's turn Neues Bauen. Today the read room has disappeared, replac by the museum shop.

26  Festschrift 1976, p. 13.
27  Jehle 1982, p. 106.
28  von Moos 2010, p. 13.
29  Festschrift 1976, p. 14.

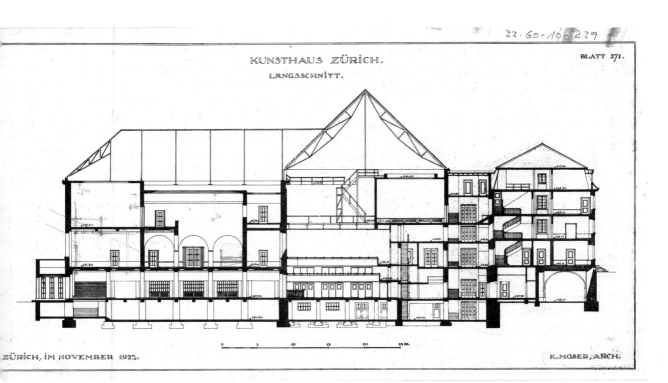

KUNSTHAUS ZÜRICH.

LÆNGSSCHNITT.

BLATT 271.

ZÜRICH, IM NOVEMBER 1925.

K.MOSER, ARCH.

Whereas the Kunsthaus of 1910 was still itself an artistic building, by the same measure the 1925 annexe is a neutral art receptacle. The ornamentation has evaporated, giving way to smoothly plastered walls that represent mere background and no longer architectural creation. The rooms were neutral, adaptable for different types of hangings, but they were still individually enclosed saloons and cabinets – nobody could yet conceive of modifying and combining them. The ceremonious quality has been replaced by a soberness. With the library and the newly built lecture hall, what previously had been a place of reverential viewing was expanded to become a house of learning. Whether, in the process, the extended Kunsthaus became a magnet to a different public including the educated classes is impossible to discern.

e facade of the extension,
h its row of fenestration that
minated the side-lit hall
works of sculpture, is the
y existing remnant of Moser's
nexe. To the left is the
ermediate building that incor-
ated the Villa Landolt.

e Villa Landolt, here shown
the right, is now integrated
hin the Kunsthaus and
entated towards Hirschen-
aben in the foreground. In the
ddle is Moser's annexe with
high glass roof, docking
to the villa 'from behind'.
the left is one of the original
torical houses.

lowing page spread:

e interior of the glass roof
ove Moser's 1925 annexe with
iew onto its counterpart
ove the Collections Building
1910. In the foreground is
dust covering above one of the
hibition rooms on the second
per floor. The stairs to the
right lead to the hollow space
ove the reading room.
image page 23, bottom.

6. V. 1925

# Another Intermezzo:
# A Modern Kunsthaus

Hardly had the annexe been completed than Moser continued with his extension plans. Between 1927 and 1935 he drafted six different designs to explore the further potential to expand. The common denominator was that all of them foresaw extending the Kunsthaus towards the Old Town, where the Pfister Building now stands. Two of them in particular are worthy of comment: the Kongresshaus (Congress Hall) and the Kammlösung (comb solution). In order to make space for the Kongresshaus while at the same time obtaining room for an expansion of the Kunsthaus, in January 1934 Moser proposed demolishing all the buildings between the Kunsthaus and Hirschengraben, including the premises today housing Pro Helvetia. The great hall of the Kongresshaus was to accommodate 3,000 people, the adjacent small hall 1,000. A restaurant was also planned. This was a futile endeavour – since 1939 the home of the Zurich Kongresshaus has been on the Guisan-Quai.

Heimplatz would have been redesigned, and even the so-called 'Zähringerdurchbruch' (the Zähringer Cut) is there in the plans, whereby the intention was to lengthen Zähringerstrasse right through the Old Town from Zähringerplatz to Heimplatz. The Zunfthaus (Guild House) on Neumarkt and the Obergericht (High Court) would have been torn down. Based on Haussmann's Paris model, the street-cut project originated in the second half of the nineteenth century and was only finally abandoned in 1942. From today's perspective what is remarkable is that already in 1934 Moser had sketched out a large gallery building on the other side of Heimplatz, precisely at the point where David Chipperfield's project has now emerged, its dimensions having a surprising affinity with Moser's scheme,[30] and Moser himself apparently never considered the two gymnastics halls as worthy of preserving.[31]

The so-called 'comb solution' of April 1934 treats the existing surrounding buildings even more ruthlessly. Not merely does Moser knock down all the houses stretching down to Hirschengraben, he even erases part of the Untere and Obere Zäune, including the upper Kirchgasse. A narrow connecting segment docks onto the Collections Building and

30  Jehle 1982, p. 114.
31  Jehle 1982, p. 114.

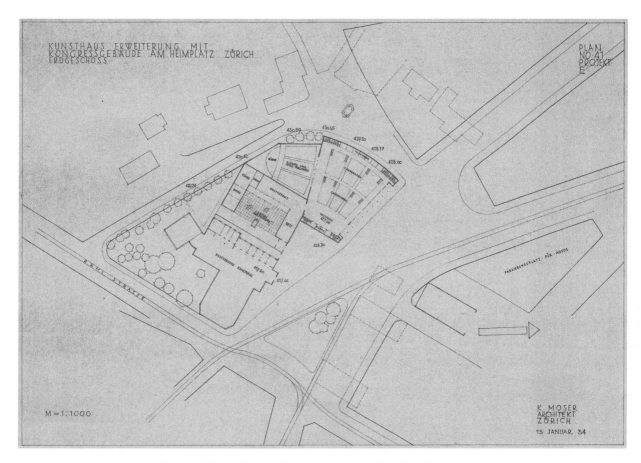

forms a screen facade facing Heimplatz. The segment is the backbone providing circulation to three transverse exhibition wings: the comb figure. The middle storey is illuminated from the side, the upper one with zenithal northern light via shed-roof fenestration. Situated on the ground floor between the teeth of the comb is a lecture hall with 1,000 seats and a restaurant. The arcade facing Heimplatz contains shops.

By the 1930s Moser was over 70, but had become a convinced proponent of Neues Bauen. With the Antonius Church in Basel in 1927 he had achieved a flagship building that set the standard for Swiss Modernism. He radically broke with his architectural past. The new designs for the extension pay no regard whatsoever to his own Kunsthaus of 1910. The neoclassical symmetry has vanished. Moser places his modern extension next to the Kunsthaus as an autonomous, innately coherent building – he is not extending something, he merely connects.

The Kongresshaus project of January 1934, there on the site where the Pfister Building now stands. The Zähringer Cut alters Heimplatz. Moser's idea was to demolish the Obergericht and part of the Untere Zäune. The gymnastics halls have to make way for the enlargement of the square.

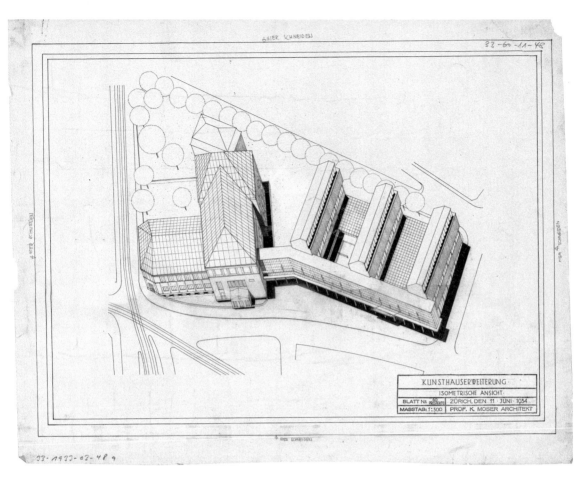

The designs of the 1930s are no longer a tailor-made sequence of rooms for an existing art collection; instead they are a neutral longitudinal hall that can be subdivided as required. There is hardly any difference between the exhibition and the collection rooms. They are all equivalent galleries or exhibition hallways, no longer a hierarchy of cabinets and saloons. The museum is seen as a factory of education – a site for the production of art schooling. Monumentality has no place here; the Kunsthaus exudes an aura of holy rationality. Quite the opposite of the new building of the Kunstmuseum Basel by Rudolf Christ and Paul Büchi, with the masterminding cooperation of Paul Bonatz, which was opened in 1936. In this case the alignment of the rooms is hierarchical, subservient to a programmatic hanging, and the building is a place of culture, symmetrical in both its layout and main facade. A palace, not an observation ward. Whether Moser's comb solution would have found favour in a referendum is admittedly doubtful.

Moser's comb solution of summ
1934 is an autonomous work
of Modern architecture that
simply docks onto the Collecti
Building rather than extending
it. The remodelled Heimplatz
is framed by a screen wall. The
baldachin marks the entrance
to the lecture hall.

# The Great Hall:
# The Pfister Building

Karl Moser's death in February 1936 in no way meant that the extension of the Kunsthaus was off the drawing board. In 1938 Director Wilhelm Wartmann drew up the construction programme for an ideas competition. In an expert opinion, the architecture professor and future chief architect of the 1939 Landesausstellung Hans Hofmann recommended an 'island of art' and to 'frame Heimplatz with a closed building development'. He espoused the creation of a large pedestrian square by partly relocating the annoying vehicle traffic. Based on this concept, new building lines were set.[32] But it would not be until 15 July 1941 that the second expansion gathered steam. This was the day that the industrial magnate Dr Emil Georg Bührle (1890–1956), owner of the Werkzeugmaschinenfabrik Oerlikon (Machine Tool Factory Oerlikon), asked to inspect the planning papers, and upon doing so made a commitment to contribute two million francs towards the building costs, which he transferred into the building fund on the spot.[33] The Building Commission, composed of the museum people and with Hofmann as a consultant, now worked quickly and by the end of 1941 had ironed out the competition programme. Retained in it was also Hofmann's closed Heimplatz. Quite naturally, with no ado, the old buildings on Krautgartenstrasse were condemned to be demolished, including the much-loved Café Östli.[34] Due to the war the competition was delayed until 1944. Participation was open to anyone who was a citizen of the Canton of Zurich or was registered as an architect, albeit not foreigners. The prize jury was made up of the architects Arthur Dürig from Basel, Otto Dreyer from Lucerne, Professor Hans Hofmann, the Chief Cantonal Architect Heinrich Peter, Kunsthaus Director Wilhelm Wartmann, Franz Meyer, the President of the Kunstgesellschaft, and Emil Georg Bührle. The verdict came on 11 May 1944. The winners were Hans and Kurt Pfister, as an office the Gebrüder Pfister (Pfister Brothers).

Although Bührle paid a further two million francs into the building fund in 1946 in order to speed up the project, construction nonetheless first began in November 1954, held up as it was by the scarcity of

32  SBZ 77/19, p. 281.
33  Linsmayer 2015, p. 132.
34  Festschrift 1976, p. 16.

materials and the priority given to housing in the immediate postwar years. A further contributing factor was the refusal of the electorate, still composed entirely of men, to grant the Kunsthaus an increased operating subsidy in 1951. Moreover, the Kunstgesellschaft itself was in a shaky financial position and had to first secure the running costs before tackling the construction of the new building. Responsibilities were thus disentangled: since 1954 the newly founded Stiftung Zürcher Kunsthaus (Kunsthaus Zürich Foundation) has been the owner of the premises and rents the Kunsthaus free of charge to the Zürcher Kunstgesellschaft, which looks after the running of it.

The breakthrough came with Bührle's offer to cover all of the costs for the new building, conditional upon the city conferring the building land to the Stiftung Zürcher Kunsthaus for nothing and assuming all the periphery costs. However, construction had to begin before the end of 1954, and if not he would retract his money. On 7 February 1954 Zurich's male population agreed to an alteration of the zoning plans and transferred the ownership of the municipal property.

Krautgartenstrasse shortly befor the demolitions; right, Moser 1. The houses in the Old Town wer little appreciated in the 1950s. 'Gentrification' was not a word in the vocabulary of those who believed so passionately in the future. The profile masts for the Pfister Building can already be seen.

All the political parties, even the communist Partei der Arbeit (Workers' Party), endorsed 'the new Kunsthaus building and the acceptance of 6 million in blood money'.[35] Blood money? Bührle manufactured weapons, which he had above all sold to Nazi Germany. On 15 November, shortly before the expiry of the ultimatum, building work started. As with all large-scale projects the opponents reacted (too) late. Their counterattack was focused less on the extension of the Kunsthaus and more on the demolition of thirteen buildings in the Old Town on Krautgartenstrasse – without success.[36]

The project of 1954 differs fundamentally from that of 1944. After the war, temporary exhibitions became increasingly more important than the main collection, which is why the new building was to serve only as an exhibition hall. For economy the volume was scaled down and for practical reasons only one entrance was planned, there where it already was in the Moser 1. In order to create a porous connection with Kirchgasse and the Old Town, the building was set on top of supports and the restaurant slotted in as a glazed box beneath. The connection to the old building was pressed backwards. The flat stairs to the Pfister Building commence only at the rear of the old foyer. The second extension of the Kunsthaus Zürich was inaugurated on 7 June 1958. Emil Georg Bührle was never able to experience the finished exhibition hall as he died in November 1956. His widow assumed his place on the Building Commission, and she was willing also to bear the entire costs of approximately 800,000 francs for the building of the restaurant,[37] designed by the architect Rudolf Zürcher.

In urban-planning terms, together with the existing Kunsthaus the protruding new building forms a corner square. Unfortunately it proved impossible 'to free the square of the through traffic from Central to Kreuzplatz; on the contrary, due to the essential alleviation of traffic flows on the Limmatquai the axis had to be accorded a greater importance. Thus only a rudiment from the original intention to create a spatially enclosed pedestrian square remained.'[38] The powerful, almost white block is a stilted container, floating above the public space with its sharp corners and lined by horizontal grooves. In the interior, on the upper floor, is a 70-metre-long, 18-metre-wide and 5-metre-high free-span hall, devoid of all partitioning. Or to be more precise:

35  Linsmayer 2015, p. 143.
36  Buomberger 2015, pp. 149 ff.
37  Buomberger 2015, p. 176.
38  SBZ 77/19, p. 281.

any form of subdivision can be undertaken, customised to match each respective exhibition. Staging an exhibition no longer entailed configuring the works to fit the existing rooms, instead it meant devising the exhibition rooms within the huge vessel. 'It is not easy to start from scratch with every exhibition, to stand with a stack of works in a completely empty space', the Director René Wehrli wrote looking back on a decade's experience.[39] The uninterrupted skylight ensures a ubiquitous lighting quality, while the two sidelight strips serve to present sculptures, although they also provide the desired opportunity to gaze outside. It was important not to lose connection with the city. As was de rigueur for the 1950s, the new exhibition hall was fully air-conditioned, driven by the largest air-conditioning system in Zurich at the time. The planners lavished particular attention on the service installations and the lighting. Energy was still cheap, and 3 centimetres of cork sufficed as heat insulation.

What the Gebrüder Pfister built was an exhibition hall not an art museum. The compositional rule behind the building is one of flexibility, thus 'adhering almost word-for-word to the strictures of classic Modernism'.[40] A functionalist receptacle with the ambition not to be artistic, but rational, not to be ostentatious, but utilitarian. The design idiom is sparse, restrained and unadorned. Like Moser's comb solution it stands self-contained but self-confidently next to the old Kunsthaus, with which it only organisationally forms a whole. Modernism had yet to fall prey to doubts. This is what an art gallery looks like at the height of the twentieth century: neutral, highly equipped, flexible. Constructed in the language of Modernist forms by people who believed in the future, who laboured for the boom-prosperity era, who stood with both feet firmly in the midst of the Cold War, and who wanted to be reminded of as few details of the recent past as possible. In 1958 the City of Zurich had 431,000 inhabitants, or 227 percent more than in 1910, including the second wave of municipal incorporations, while the Kunstgesellschaft now boasted 2,875 members.

Moser's reading room disappeared with the Pfister Building. Ceilings were inserted in Moser 3 to create more space for the collection. The Kunsthaus Zürich was now equipped to join in the emerging carousel of major temporary exhibitions. Within Switzerland the

Section, plan and view of the exterior wall. For now, any interest in heat insulation was still almost negligible – the gigantic air-conditioning syste extracted hot air in summer and heated in winter. The dus ceiling can be walked on, and vertical blinds regulate the lig

39 200 Jahre 1987.
40 Jehle 1982, p. 133.

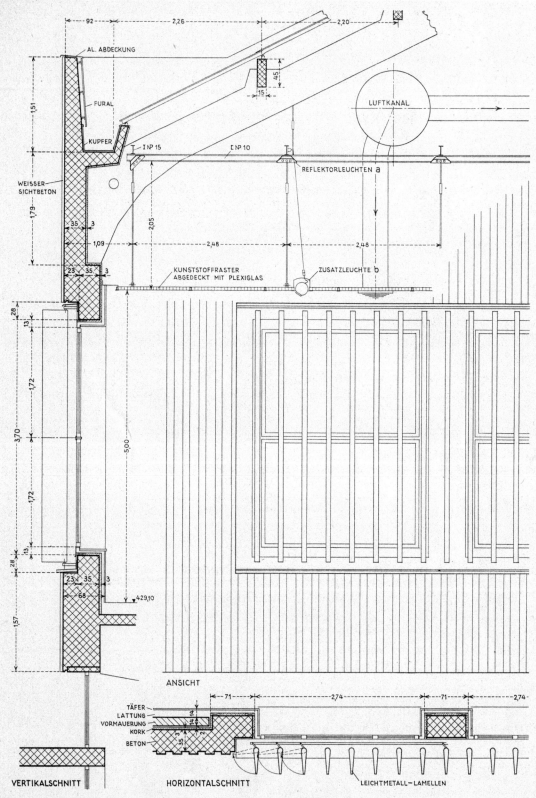

AL. ABDECKUNG

FURAL

KUPFER

WEISSER
SICHTBETON

LUFTKANAL

I NP 15

I NP 10

REFLEKTORLEUCHTEN a

KUNSTSTOFFRASTER
ABGEDECKT MIT PLEXIGLAS

ZUSATZLEUCHTE b

429,10

ANSICHT

VERTIKALSCHNITT

HORIZONTALSCHNITT

TÄFER
LATTUNG
VORMAUERUNG
KORK
BETON

LEICHTMETALL–LAMELLEN

Neuer Ausstellungssaal, Schnitt und Ansicht der Aussenwand 1:60

Pfister Building also had a smaller sibling, the Aargauer Kunsthaus by the architects Loepfe, Hänni, Hänggli, completed in 1959, as well as an even smaller sibling in the form of the 1952 Kunsthaus Glarus by the architect Hans Leuzinger. Nevertheless, newly constructed museums were rare in Switzerland at the time. The most contemporary of the Pfister Building's generation, and a Modernist icon, is the Neue Nationalgalerie in Berlin, a late work of Mies van der Rohe's from 1968. Likewise worth recalling is the Guggenheim Museum by Frank Lloyd Wright in New York, completed in 1959 – a contemporary of the Pfister Building in which everything is the complete opposite, namely where art serves architecture and not vice versa.

Internally the Pfister Building a neutral, free-span exhibition hall that can be spatially divid up as needed. The full-length zenithal lighting supplies a ste ubiquitous light. The picture shows the situation following the renovations of 2005.

The Pfister Building of 1959, together with the Kunsthaus, forms a public corner that frames Heimplatz on one side The stand-alone block suppon on columns merges with the Moserbau in terms of organi- sation. Between the buildings is a garden courtyard.

# What to do with Heimplatz?

In the 1960s the City of Zurich set about planning a solution to the surge in private motorised traffic – an engineering marvel called the 'City Ring'. The high-capacity, motorway-like ring road was to bypass the Old Town, as well as providing access to the requisite parking garages, at approximately the point where the Baroque fortification entrenchments had been. In this scheme Heimplatz was to become a node in the City Ring, reconstructed to form a carefully thought-out gigantic traffic infrastructure with road lanes set on multiple levels. The aim was to achieve a 'traffic-free zone between the Kunsthaus and the Schauspielhaus',[41] all the more opportune since from 1964 onwards the Schauspielhaus theatre opposite the museum had been waiting for work to begin on a new building planned by Jørn Utzon – a project that in the end never came about.[42] The Kunsthaus and the new Schauspielhaus building would have formed a pedestrian island in the midst of roaring traffic. Heimplatz would have become an enclosed urban space – more modest than Hofmann had originally planned, but at least a pedestrian square to stop and pause for a while.

The City Ring would have freed Heimplatz of traffic, or to be more precise would have created a pedestrian island surrounded by roaring traffic. Opposite the Kunsthaus, where the Chipperfield Building now stands, are blueprints of a project for a new Schauspielhaus by Jørn Utzon

41  City-Ring 1967, p. 6.
42  Neubau Schauspielhaus 1964.

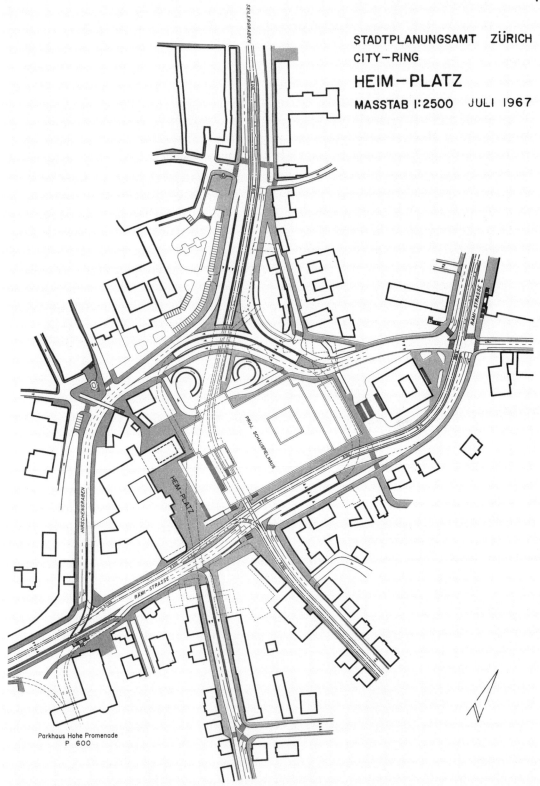

4

STADTPLANUNGSAMT ZÜRICH
CITY—RING

# HEIM—PLATZ

MASSTAB 1:2500    JULI 1967

PROJ. SCHAUSPIELHAUS

HEIM-PLATZ

RÄMI-STRASSE

HIRSCHENGRABEN

SEILERGRABEN

Parkhaus Hohe Promenade
P 600

# Duck Down:
# The Müller Building

Despite the recent extension the Kunsthaus soon suffered from a renewed shortage of space. 'For this reason it was highly welcome that Frau Dr H. E. Mayenfisch and Herr Dr A. Schäfer decided to donate to us a new gallery, above all for French paintings. This gallery was erected by the architect Bruno Giacometti above the connecting segment between the old and the new buildings so as to join onto the collection rooms on the second floor of the old building. [...] A visitors' roof terrace provides not only an opportunity to enjoy the views but also to exhibit sculptures.'[43] This so-called 'Seerosensaal' (Water Lilies Gallery), in which Claude Monet's huge water lilies paintings were hung, was completed in 1968. With the major renovation of 2002 it would quietly disappear. It blocked a goods lift, muddled the connection between the Moser and Pfister Buildings, and was overall structurally barely savable.

Frau Olga Mayenfisch was a faithful patroness. In summer 1969 she donated seven million francs to the Stiftung Zürcher Kunsthaus for a third extension. She did so in 'lasting remembrance of her deceased husband. As long-standing Vice-President of the Zürcher Kunstgesell-schaft, Herr Hans E. Mayenfisch had earned enormous merit on behalf of the Kunsthaus Zürich, to whom he also donated an important collection of contemporary Swiss paintings.'[44] Thus, in October 1969 the City Council announced a public competition. This time the aim was to build behind and not beside the existing complex, in the garden between Rämistrasse and Hirschengraben. The Villa Landolt was condemned to be demolished. The talk was of a 'final expansion of the Kunsthaus Zürich'.[45] The jury consisted of Building Chairman, Dept. 2, Edwin Frech, the President of the Zürcher Kunstgesellschaft Alfred Schaefer, Kunsthaus Director René Wehrli, the architects Bruno Giacometti, Manfred Lehmbruck and Jacques Schader, the Basel Chief Cantonal Architect Hans Luder and Chief Municipal Architect Adolf Wasserfallen. The winner was declared in May 1970: Erwin Müller (1925–2017) and his collaborator Heinrich Blumer from Zurich.

The roof terrace above the connecting building was a view platform and a sculpture gard in one. The view opened out onto one of the two gymnastic halls – this one built by the Ch Municipal Building Inspector Otto Weber in 1880 – that later had to make way for the Chipperfield Building.

43  Jahresbericht 1968, p. 9.
44  Festschrift 1976, p. 26.
45  Jehle 1982, p. 133.

Following the Oil Crisis of 1973 the previous euphoria evaporated. City President Sigmund Widmer ruefully admitted, 'Terms like extension and expansion are not exactly words with a wholly positive ring to them at the moment', but nevertheless set about the task of 'giving more detailed reasons' for a third extension 'for the attention of a wider public'.[46] The self-confident movers and shakers felt a pressure to justify themselves. Their answer was an architectural ducking exercise. Seen from Heimplatz and from Rämistrasse the extension is hardly visible. Müller arranged three polygonal architectural volumes, staggered in height, in a row next to each other. The already existing access ramp to the Hohe Promenade parking garage runs diagonally upwards in front of it. In essence the building sits at the back on the left. On the ground-floor level a passageway leads underneath through the building, connecting Hirschengraben with Rämistrasse – a little-used amenity. The passageway was also the entrance to the newly installed Kunsthaus Library. Three shops and a café were created on Rämistrasse, including ten window display cases set in the retaining wall. It was an attempt to enliven the bleakness of Rämistrasse: small businesses instead of the all-pervading wall. But whoever crosses Rämistrasse nowadays sees little of the Kunsthaus and nothing of the Müller Building. First of all, the start of the extension is set back behind a retaining garden wall, and secondly commences two storeys higher up, which only adds to the effect. Anyone who is inquisitive enough can, if they want, fight their way through the run-down garden that lies like a neglected terrace above Rämistrasse. The trees that stand here were deliberately preserved – for once they were more important than the building. Moser, and the Gebrüder Pfister too, would have felled them without batting an eyelid if they had stood in the way of their projects, but by now people were more sensitised – cutting down trees had become an ecological sin. Not so the Villa Landolt, which disappeared. Standing in the garden one can also see Moser's disciplined facade, or at least what of the 1926 extension still remains in its original state.

Müller's extension is a layered solution. The exhibition spaces are spread out over three floors, jutting outwards one above another like opened drawers. Architects term this 'flowing space', while museum professionals shake their heads and insert dividing walls. 'There is an unintentional dramatic feeling – perspectives, corners, openings and

46 Festschrift 1976, p. 27.

gradations in height – that detract from the content, from the art. The technical sophistication of the lighting is so completely predominant that the way it is orchestrated clashes with the exhibition items.'[47] Nobody was truly happy with the third extension. It has a curiously non-architectural quality to it, crouching down into the slope of the hill, where it avoids attracting attention to itself – an altogether odd behaviour for a public building. The whole force of the design is concentrated on allowing the maximum possible amount of natural zenithal light into the rooms. The lighting machinery in the museum becomes rampant. In this respect a comparative glance at Bern is educational. It was here, a short time afterwards, in 1983, that Atelier 5 realised an art museum extension with the aim of 'being the most perfect backdrop possible for what happens in this house'.[48] Despite this restraint, the lighting in this case is made into a compositional principle in the museum. The ingenious light directors and light funnels from the Bartenbach light-planning firm in Innsbruck transform the museum into a veritable light machine. Nevertheless, 'in the process it was forgotten that the beholder is more important than the light. And he does not appreciate it at all when a dark, low ceiling flattens his feelings.'[49] Admittedly daylight is vital in an art museum, but nevertheless architecture re-mains the art of creating space.

The guiding museum of this generation is the Centre Pompidou in Paris by Renzo Piano and Richard Rogers, opened in 1977. Here the museum itself is a machine. The contradiction in their architectural stances between the two museums could hardly be more extreme: in Zurich the head is ducked, in Paris it is raised in Gallic self-confidence. The Müller Building is a museum of the insecure. In 1976 Zurich had 383,000 inhabitants, in other words 11 percent fewer than in 1958; the Kunstgesellschaft had 4,345 members.

Following pages:

The Müller Building of 1976 fills the triangle between Hirschen-graben to the left and Moser 3 in the middle. It stands set back, two storeys higher than Rämi-strasse. A series of window display cases and a handful of shops have been built to enliven the street.

If it is true that a space should be read via its ceiling, then in this case it is above all the sophisticated lighting techniques that define the interior of the Müller Building. The downward stepping of the roofs and the drawer-like levels demonstrate the core idea – a layered solution.

47  Jehle 1982, p. 134.
48  Kunstmuseen 1995, p. 16.
49  Mitteilungen Kunstgesellschaft 3/91, p. 12.

# The Feasibility Study

In the meantime Moser's old building had become a patient in need of remedy. The facade, roof, technical services and security system badly required modernisation. 'Parallel to the renovation it would be preferable to also achieve an enlargement of the exhibition floor space. [...] Extensions should therefore be obtained via a better consolidation of the existing Kunsthaus and within the parameters of its own grounds.'[50] Three architectural offices were invited to submit proposals: Mario Campi, Lugano, Willi Egli, Zurich, and Katharina and Wilfrid Steib, Basel. The evaluation committee was composed of: City Councillor Ursula Koch, Felix Baumann, Director of the Kunsthaus, Thomas W. Bechtler, President of the Zürcher Kunstgesellschaft, Heiri Gross, President of the Stiftung Zürcher Kunsthaus, the art historian Stanislaus von Moos, the architects Jacques Schader and Theo Hotz, and the Chief Municipal Architect Hans Rudolf Rüegg. Absent from the jury was City President Thomas Wagner. Within the group dynamics of the city government he and Councillor Koch had failed to find a consensus, leading to brief polemics in the press[51] and a deadlock between autumn 1989 and spring 1990.

Campi's project placed a bold new building in front of the Müller Building on Rämistrasse and reconstituted the reading room, or to be more precise proposed a central hall where one had once been, leading to a large set of stairs and thus dispensing with Moser's main stairway. The jury commented: 'It is regrettable that there is a failure to harmonise the suggested monumental spatial sequence with the spatial and circulation structure of the Moserbau.'[52] Katharina and Wilfrid Steib's submission similarly envisioned a new building on Rämistrasse. To achieve this they proposed demolishing part of the Müller Building, prompting the jury to ask 'Whether the proposed measures represent a sensible quid pro quo for the financial costs?'[53] In consolation, at least a critic confirmed that 'art comes before architecture for the Steibs'.[54]

Willi Egli placed a five-storey, crescent-shaped tower in the vacant space between the Pfister Building and the Haus zum Kiel on the Hirschengraben. The final completion in his version involved an additional stage, allowing him to keep the potential to expand on

How to enlarge? Top: Mario Campi positions an annexe next to the Müller Building. Middle: Wilfrid and Katharina Steib likewise extend on Rämistrasse but tear down part of the Müller Building. Bottom: Willi Egli expands the Kunsthaus with a crescent-shaped tower next to the Haus zum Kiel and vertically extends the Pfister Building with an additional exhibition storey. With the deployment of four 'light machines' the Bührle Gallery is still naturally lit from above.

50  Studienauftrag 1989, p. 1.
51  See for instance Züri Woche, 1 March 1990.
52  Bericht 1989, p. 6.
53  Bericht 1989, p. 11.
54  Strebel 1990, p. 18.

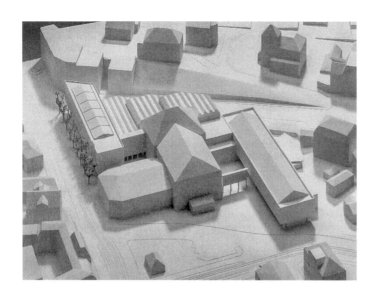

Rämistrasse as a later reserve. An extra exhibition floor was placed on top of the Pfister Building, which stole light from the Bührle Gallery, remedied by means of four large 'light machines', conceived by the Bartenbach firm, that pierced through the new heightening.

The winner was Willi Egli. 'Based on its overall quality' the jury recommended 'taking this project as the basis for the extension and refurbishment of the old building'[55] and to push forwards with Egli. Nevertheless, adapting of the plans became bogged down. While Egli drew up variations and improvements and integrated the newly acquired Villa Tobler into the project, Heiri Gross, as President of the Stiftung Zürcher Kunsthaus, contracted the architect Willy Leins with the ongoing renovation works, even though the feasibility study encompassed both the renovation and the expansion. Tensions between representatives from the Kunsthausstiftung and Egli grew, until finally, in 1996, work with Egli halted: the foundation board decided to realise the further remodelling and renovation project with the architects Schnebli Ammann Ruchat with Tobias Ammann in charge.[56] An expansion of the Kunsthaus on its own site petered out.

55  Bericht 1989, p. 13
56  Letter Thomas Wagner (president of the board of trustees) to Willi Egli, 4 July 1996.

# The Administration Moves House: Villa Tobler

He could certainly afford it. In 1855 Zurich's most important private banker, Jakob Emil Tobler-Finsler, employed Gustav Albert Wegmann, the architect of the first Kunsthaus Zürich, to build him a late-classical villa up on the mountain on the highest point of the right-hand moraine hill at Winkelwiese 4. The bank occupied the first floor, above it the apartment in which the widower and his two sons were housed. Gustav Adolf Tobler-Blumer (1850–1923), who outlived his father and his brother, did not want to become a banker, but rather a communications engineer, in the end advancing to become a professor at ETH Zurich. He dissolved the bank and used his inheritance to fundamentally remodel the house, commissioning Hans Heinrich Conrad von Muralt to do the work, assisted by Gustav Gull. 'With a few precise additions', von Muralt 'transformed the strictly classical block into a picturesque villa according to Böcklin's tastes'.[57] The interior fittings and fixtures, however, were designed by Hans Eduard von Berlepsch-Valendas (1849–1921), a student friend of Tobler's from their time together at the Zürcher Industrieschule (Zurich Industrial College). He created the lavish Jugendstil interior, the most beautiful of its kind in Zurich. Besides von Berlepsch-Valendas, another unknown Jugendstil artist was involved. Only the smoking lounge, a late-Gothic parlour, follows a historical style, responding to the client's wish to reproduce what he had previously seen in the National Museum – 'true prototypes of homeliness'.[58] After Gustav Adolf's death his son remodelled the villa a third time, preferring neo-Renaissance forms. Thus the villa embodies three styles: neoclassicism, Jugendstil, neo-Renaissance.[59]

In 1951 the property was bought by a general contractor with the intention of tearing it down, leading to opposition in the neighbourhood. In 1964 the city was able to purchase the villa, together with the garden. It was subsequently used by the Theater Heddy Maria Wettstein and the Schauspielakademie (Acting Academy), who in 1996 moved to Gessnerallee, whereupon the city entrusted the now-empty villa under property law to the Zürcher Kunstgesellschaft on condition that they defrayed the renovation costs of nine million francs.

57  Sondernummer 1995, p. 4.
58  Sondernummer 1995, p. 9.
59  Magazin 1/17, pp. 35 ff.

Following a painstaking restoration by the architect Felix Stemmle, overseen by officials from the built heritage conservation department, the Kunsthaus administration moved into the Villa Tobler on 1 July 2000.

Not only is the villa an architectural monument, but its garden too is a Listed Object of Cantonal Significance. Of particular note are the dragon basin with golden mosaics, the round Fontaine fountain and the sculpture of a youth by Richard Kissling under the pergola. The garden today is open to the public.

# The Upgrade:
# The Root-and-Branch Overhaul

Any idea of a final completion of the Kunsthaus was out of the question as long as the collection continued to grow and as long as the temporary exhibitions continually became larger and more important. Added to this, the service installations became increasingly outdated and in need of replacement. In 1984 the parquet flooring in the Müller Building had already been replaced with sisal carpet. The first phase in the renewals was the exterior renovation of the Moserbau by the architects Willy Leins and Gerold Reiser, which was completed in 1989. Parallel to Willi Egli's extension planning, but independently of it, the same two architects undertook the second phase, finished in 1991: the interior renovations of the top storey of the Moserbau, and above all the glazed roofs, focusing for the time being on the light-diffusing ceilings. Any discussion about roofs in an art museum always means also talking about light. Originally the museum was only open during the day, so the illumination was almost always daylight. Artificial lighting was not intended for the benefit of the visitors, but instead for the custodial and janitorial work. Later, ad hoc solutions had been resorted to, but now the time had come for a fundamental modernisation. The best illumination is daylight. The best daylight comes from directly above, in other words through the roof. Daylight incorporates the whole spectrum of visible wavelengths in infinitely fine gradients, but with fluorescent tubes the nuances are very uneven. Most paintings were painted by daylight and want to be viewed the same way. Diffused ceiling light cancels out irritating reflections and all of the walls are left free for hangings, which museum staff value highly. This is why curators love ceiling-light galleries, above all the old-fashioned ones with tapered haunches between the ceiling and the walls. The painter Markus Lüpertz summarised the point thus: 'The classic museum is a built affair: four walls, rooflight, two doors – one to enter through, one to depart through.'[60] The tapered haunch was reintroduced by James Stirling in the Neue Staatsgalerie Stuttgart in 1982.

Nevertheless, light cannot simply be allowed to pour in; it has to be adjustable, in other words amenable to dosing. An oil painting is most clearly viewable at a light intensity of 500 lux. However, conservators prefer less than this because light energy speeds up the process of deterioration of the pictures. The sun for its part delivers up to 100,000 lux, and that irregularly throughout the course of the day and depending on the cloud cover. On gloomy winter days and in the evening hours, any light whatsoever is greatly appreciated, whereas on a sunny midday it is far too bright. Moser dosed the light using horizontal roller blinds above the dust ceiling, which had to be operated by hand. They had long since become frayed, discoloured and dirty, and were replaced by installing new horizontal, 40-centimetre-wide slats that are rotatable. Positioned flat, hardly any daylight penetrates through, meaning the galleries can be darkened; positioned upright, light flows almost freely into the room. When closed they can additionally serve as reflectors for the artificial lighting mounted between the slats and the dust ceiling. The new control system enables the corresponding ideal lighting for the paintings in each individual gallery.

Skylighting entails a glazed roof – and glazed roofs have a tendency to become leaky. In the past it had sometimes rained into the Kunsthaus. Moreover, the giant glazed pyramids became furnaces in summer and iceboxes in winter, meaning that the room temperatures and the air humidity in the galleries fluctuated far more than was bearable – for the visitors and likewise the pictures. Any museum that wants to keep pace with the international exchange of pictures has to guarantee the light, temperature and humidity thresholds demanded by the loaners and the insurers. Security is a similarly important issue. Therefore it was a pressing priority to overhaul the building-service installations in order for the Kunsthaus Zürich to keep playing in the top league – internationally of course.

The solution is called a cold roof. The climatic barrier is no longer in the roof membrane but in the ceiling above the exhibition galleries, which are solidly insulated. The huge space beneath the glazed roof is neither heated nor cooled. Newly built-in opaque glass panels reduce the light and heat input by up to 50 percent. In winter the existing central heating warms the rooms. Because the warm air is no longer

The roof refrigerator: slats all the light to be dosed, while the dual-panel above the air-conditioned and cooled cavity space forms the climatic barri Ingoing air flows through the ceiling cooling system; outgoi air is extracted at the foot of the wall.

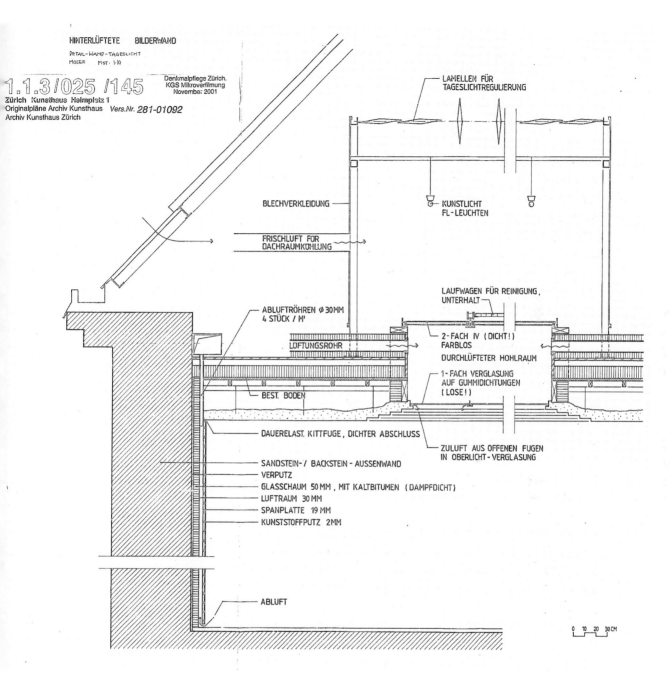

HINTERLÜFTETE BILDERWAND

DETAIL-WAND - TAGESLICHT
MOSER    MST. 1:10

LAMELLEN FÜR
TAGESLICHTREGULIERUNG

BLECHVERKLEIDUNG

KUNSTLICHT
FL-LEUCHTEN

FRISCHLUFT FÜR
DACHRAUMKÜHLUNG

LAUFWAGEN FÜR REINIGUNG,
UNTERHALT

ABLUFTRÖHREN ∅ 30MM
4 STÜCK / M'

2-FACH IV (DICHT!)
FARBLOS

DURCHLÜFTETER HOHLRAUM

LÜFTUNGSROHR

1-FACH VERGLASUNG
AUF GUMMIDICHTUNGEN
(LOSE!)

BEST. BODEN

DAUERELAST. KITTFUGE, DICHTER ABSCHLUSS

ZULUFT AUS OFFENEN FUGEN
IN OBERLICHT-VERGLASUNG

SANDSTEIN-/ BACKSTEIN - AUSSENWAND
VERPUTZ
GLASSCHAUM 50MM, MIT KALTBITUMEN (DAMPFDICHT)
LUFTRAUM 30MM
SPANPLATTE 19MM
KUNSTSTOFFPUTZ 2MM

ABLUFT

0  10  20  30CM

53

lost via the ceiling and the roof, the room temperature remains constant. Humidity is controlled using precisely applied fresh-air intake. In summer cooling is provided by the 'roof refrigerator'. A cavity space between the dust ceiling and the glazed layer above it is flushed out using cold air, thus discharging any excess warmth. On hot days the glazed roofs can be opened and a ventilator forces out the warm air underneath the pyramids. The air-conditioning plant is housed in the cellar, necessitating the installation of two new riser shafts between Moser's Collections Building (Moser 1) and the 1926 extension (Moser 3), and which are cleverly concealed within a thickening of the walls.

The third and fourth phases, known as the 'major renovation', lasted from 1997 until 2005. Although the Kunsthausstiftung was happy with Willy Leins's work, his office was nevertheless too small to cope with the major renovation and the architect Tobias Ammann from the office sam (Schnebli Ammann Menz) was put in charge. On 24 September 2001 Zurich's voters authorised 28 million francs in municipal funds towards the total building costs of 55 million, 80 percent of which represented investments in the service installations and as such was essentially invisible.

Ammann presented a concept and a trial run was undertaken on a sample room: what had the interior of Moser's Kunsthaus originally looked like in 1910? The renovations themselves commenced in September 2001, starting with the Exhibition Wing (Moser 2). The relocation of the administration to the Villa Tobler had freed up the rooms on the ground floor and these were now rearranged to hold the works of Alberto Giacometti (1901–1966).

Most people who were around at the time remember the events: Giacometti's works in the Kunsthaus belong to the Alberto Giacometti-Stiftung, which came about as a result of the so-called 'Zurich Art Controversy' that raged in the newspaper columns in spring 1965. The bone of contention was a municipal purchase credit for a collection of works by Giacometti, prompting two camps with opposing outlooks on art, each with their own figureheads, to clash swords. On the one side was the frondeur Peter Meyer, the forcefully vocal professor of art history, who opposed the credit in the name of common sense and sanity. On the other side the networker of Modernism Carola Giedion-Welcker, who supported the purchase in the name of enlightenment and progress. The City Parliament rejected the credit, whereupon the supporters created the Alberto Giacometti-Stiftung, which ultimately bought the works and put them on show in the Kunsthaus. A later gift enlarged the size of the inventory.

Tobias Ammann set an artificially lit gallery in the centre of the ground floor of the Exhibition Wing (Moser 2), conceived for the light-sensitive graphic works. Around it he placed a loop of four cabinets with side lighting. 'Sculptures essentially exist from light, and this particularly applies to Giacometti's works. The light should neither be blurred, nor should it come from above; on the contrary it should preferably come from a higher-level side source, just like Giacometti himself used in his studio.'[61] Three existing columns were surgically removed, allowing a free-span central gallery. The suspended ceiling smoothes over the differing ceiling heights in the Böcklin and Fuseli Galleries above. Ammann paid particular attention to the bases for the works of art – 'a tricky and repeatedly discussed element'.[62]

Giacometti's works had initially been presented in the Villa Landolt, after its demolition in the Müller Building, and since 2002 'as a pleasing, enclosed area'[63] in the remodelled rooms in the Exhibition Wing. However, with the start of the Chipperfield Building the ground floor had to be closed to enable the construction of the underground passageway and Giacometti was transplanted to various floors of the Müller Building. Once completed, Giacometti will in future appear in the first upper floor of the Chipperfield Building. 'There are more contained spatial segments available there, which will once again make other facets of the work of the monumental artists experiencable.'[64]

The Pfister Building likewise underwent renovations. The acrylic patterning on the ceiling had yellowed, and this was inflammable, too. In this case roller blinds in the roof slope control the amount of incoming light. For financial reasons the building services had been omitted from the modernisation programme in the Müller Building. During the entire building schedule the museum had had to stay open, which meant that the work had to be carried out in stages.

61 Sondernummer 1995, p. 12.
62 Neue Räume 2002, p. 8.
63 Magazin 2/17, p. 34.
64 Magazin 1/17, p. 35.

By the end of it the Kunsthaus had now been transformed into a lighting and air-conditioning machine – computer-guided, intelligent and, naturally, fully automated. 'For the first time in half a century, at least above the picture mountings the rooms are able to present themselves in a worthy state again,'[65] commented curator Christian Klemm in 2001. Not only was the service infrastructure brought up-to-date but the original decor had been rediscovered. In the 90 years since its construction much of the early substance of the building had been lost or covered up. Moser himself had initiated this process in 1926 and had whitewashed over his own ancient-oriental version of the plaster mouldings in the stairway hall. 'In keeping with the principle of a superior artistic value that can be unequivocally attributed to the original state'[66] these 'corrections' were reversed. The restorers also discovered the original carpeting in historical photographs and had it newly woven again. The only part to be reorganised was the entrance area: the shop and the cloakroom are pushed deeper into the building, giving the museum café and the ticket desk more room. Whoever visits the Kunsthaus nowadays notices none of the complicated service installations and gives little thought to the superior quality of light, and indeed the real accomplishment of the architects and technicians is that all of this appears so matter-of-fact. The restoration was completed on 26 October 2005.[67] As a final act the library in the Müller Building moved premises to Rämistrasse, where previously the café and the shop had been housed, swapping rooms with the Collection of Prints and Drawings.

Something was still missing – the glazed roofs. They were leaky and the fluctuations in humidity in the cold roof lead to condensation and consequently the corrosion of the century-old steel sections. The structural safety began to dwindle; the rusted steel sections had to be replaced and those that were still stable had to be newly coated. The architect was fully aware 'that the proposed approach would not completely solve the problem. More value was attached to the conservational requirements placed on the object than a state-of-the-art resolution of the problem.'[68] Nevertheless, he noted, at least the glazed roof survived Storm Lothar. The works were carried out in summer 2014, whereby it was possible to reuse almost all of the old glass panels.

As far as possible the major renovation saw a return to the original state of the buildin The carpeting, for example, was newly woven based on old photographs. The greatest achievement of the architects a conservationists is that everything appears so natural.

65  Mitteilungen der Kunstgesellschaft 3/01, p. 12.
66  Mitteilungen der Kunstgesellschaft 3/01, p. 14.
67  Hasche 2006, pp. 23 ff.
68  Letter Ammann Architekten to the district architect, 17 October 2013.

# The Third Kunsthaus:
# The Chipperfield Building

As the feasibility study had already shown, a plausible fourth enlargement on the scale that had become needed was impossible on the existing site. Moreover, the intention was to incorporate the Emil Bührle Collection within the Kunsthaus. A third art museum had become essential. But where? One did not have to cast one's gaze far. Opposite the Kunsthaus lay the canton-owned property that Karl Moser had already included in his extension projects in the 1930s. It belonged to the ensemble of the old Kantonsschule (Cantonal School) by Gustav Adolf Wegmann, erected in 1842 on the Rämibollwerk (Rämi Bastion) and supplemented in 1880 (by Buildings Inspector Otto Weber) and 1902 (by Kehrer & Knell) with two gymnastics halls. Over time the park, which leads up from Heimplatz to the palazzo of the Kantonsschule, had become cluttered with school huts and was hardly appreciable as such. However, the ensemble was listed. The city authorities, who assumed the lead role, were well aware of the risks involved and from the very start proceeded with caution. Deploying a mixture of test planning and workshops they sounded out all of the obstacles and disposed of them. The perimeter was restricted, not least because of fears of stumbling across the ruins of the Baroque town fortifications and the traces of a suspected Jewish graveyard. As is also the case with such projects nowadays, the architects had to cater for an over-dimensional programme on an under-dimensional plot of land. It 'reads like an insurance policy',[69] commented Hochparterre Wettbewerbe wryly. Expressed in other terms: the design corset was tightly laced.

In November 2008 the anonymous competition was judged in a selective process. Of the 180 applicants, 20 architecture offices were chosen to participate, carefully chosen from across the Western world. The approach created a murmur of discontent among the Federation of Swiss Architects (FSA), who would have preferred to see an open competition held. Those invited included major names such as David Chipperfield, Caruso St John, Josep Lluís Mateo and Grazioli/ Krischanitz, but also the crème de la crème of Swiss architecture, ranging from Diener & Diener, Max Dudler, Gigon/Guyer, Meili Peter

69 Hochparterre Wettbewerbe 1/09, p. 5.

and Miller & Maranta to mazzapokora and pool. Besides the official Zurich government representatives, the prize jury was composed of the architects Francine M. J. Houben from Delft, Hilde Léon from Berlin, Laurids Ortner from Vienna and Emanuel Christ from Basel, as well as Norbert Zimmermann from the Stiftung Preussischer Kulturbesitz (Prussian Cultural Heritage Foundation), Maja Oeri from the Laurenz Foundation, Theodora Vischer from Schaulager, the artist Peter Fischli, the President of the Zürcher Kunstgesellschaft Walter B. Kielholz and the Kunsthaus Director Christoph Becker. The moderation of the whole was supervised by Professor Carl Fingerhuth. 'The Kunsthaus Zürich plays an important cultural role in positioning Zurich among world's metropolises', stated the prize jury's report,[70] and this international focus was underscored by choice of the jury members and the participants. The aim was an ambitious one: the 'Museum of the Twenty-First Century', obviously at the same time fulfilling the standards of the 2000-Watt Society.[71] The connection between the old and the new building had to be planned under the ground – any potential remodelling of Heimplatz was put off until the future. What Hofmann had already attempted in 1938 was circumspectly postponed. The aim was to find a solution for a museum not a public square. Combining the new building with the burden of the intractable traffic problem would have sunk the boat, or to put it bluntly would have been shipwrecked at the ballot box. The popular 'no' to Moneo's Kongresshaus was still ringing in the ears of those responsible. Urban development is about winning the vote.

The winner was David Chipperfield Architects, Berlin. Chipperfield places a powerful, uninterrupted cube on Heimplatz – in terms of its floor plan almost a square measuring 60 metres along its edges and 21 metres in height. In the future the architectural centre of attraction of the Kunsthaus lies on the other side of the square. The cube, which dominates its surroundings, finally frames the urban environs of the public space. Simultaneously the new building as a block is an answer to that of old Kantonsschule. Between the two palazzi will be an art garden. 'By virtue of its assimilation within the historical site the architectural expression remains ... relatively conservative and restrained', wrote the prize jury, which also faulted its 'already criticised fascination with historicism' in its facade. The museum of the twenty-

70  Hochparterre Wettbewerbe 1/09, p. 5.
71  Hochparterre Wettbewerbe 1/09, p. 5.

first century mirrors its nineteenth-century predecessor, which is entirely understandable looking back on the architectural escapades in museum building over the previous decades. Un retour à l'ordre. Everywhere is not Bilbao. The mute mass generates a silent grandeur alone through its sheer weight. This is what monumentality looks like today. Chipperfield asserts the primacy of the museum as a civic, or to be precise, valuable building on the strength of its ability to communicate values. Art, that great other, requires a symbolic vessel. 'It's obvious that I long ago replaced the church with the museum', wrote Harald Szeemann on the subject.[72] A panorama of recent Swiss museum buildings can help to provide a categorisation. The Vitra Design Museum by Frank Gehry sets an explanation mark that can be seen from afar: an architectural tour de force, but not simple to choreograph, to put it mildly. The Museum Tinguely by Mario Botta has a spectacular viewing balcony facing the River Rheine, but other than that is more a conventional art container with lighting that is difficult to manage. Schaulager by Herzog & de Meuron combines rationality with the pathos of tall space, its facade facing the city obliged to make a bold statement in an otherwise industrial zone. The Fondation Beyeler building by Renzo Piano is a shrine to art in a park – restful, rich and romantic. The Zentrum Paul Klee, likewise by Piano, encases a thoroughly rational layout within the arbitrary form of its three waves. This list does not even include the numerous new art gallery complexes that have sprung up like mushrooms across the globe, but one thing is evident: 'anything goes' is a maxim that applies also to museum building. Chipperfield, for his part, counters these types with an encased block – a 'Classical-order fastening'. As already clearly expressed in his reconstruction of the Neues Museum in Berlin and the Museum of Modern Literature (LiMo) in Marbach, his fascination with Historicism is in fact a form of Classicism. As Sigfried Giedion observed in 1922: 'Classicism is not a style. Classicism is colouration.'[73] The new house will undoubtedly have a persistence of presence.

'The arrangement of the exhibition spaces, the management of the visitor flows, as well as the operational organisation are persuasive.'[74] The backbone of this inner organisation is a hall that slices through the architectural volume following the gradient of the hill and pierces all of the storeys. It also connects Heimplatz with the art garden, which is

72  Mack 1999, p. 10.
73  Giedion 1922, p. 9.
74  All quotes from these two sections from: Report by the Prize Jury, 1964.

located a storey higher and stretches up to the old Kantonsschule. Whether the hall can equally connect Heimplatz and the art garden as public space is more doubtful. There are good reasons to go into the Kunsthaus, but fewer reasons to go through it. Situated on both sides of the hall are the exhibition galleries. Chipperfield conceives them as rooms for contemplation. 'What I mean by this is that we should not forget the role of the museum as a place of retreat; as a place where we can find stillness.'[75] On the ground floor are the educational rooms and the ceremonial hall. The bar and the second museum shop open out onto Heimplatz. The hall has a dual effect: an exhalation or expanse and to provide access routes. It possesses the quality that Moser avoided and that Campi wanted to introduce into the old building: the pathos of lofty space, which is reinforced by the upward sweep of the monumental stairway at the end of the hall. Up above, at a height of almost 18 metres, the central skylight floats over the visitors. This hall is magnificent: great in its nature and great in its type. This time around the dimensions are no longer liberal–republican, rather internationally competitive. In 2020 Zurich will have an estimated 435,000 inhabitants (middle scenario of the Statistics Office) and the Kunstgesellschaft some 22,000 members. Between 1910 and 2020 Switzerland's capital of business has become a global city – Zurich the metropolis. The hall embodies this ascendency. The cost-ceiling for the new building has been set at 206 million francs: 88 million approved by the city's voters, a further 88 million from the Zürcher Kunstgesellschaft (or to be more precise its members, benefactors, foundations and sponsors) and a final 30 million from the Lottery Fund.[76]

Once the competition was over, work promptly began on refining the project. The City of Zurich, the Stiftung Zürcher Kunsthaus and the Zürcher Kunstgesellschaft founded the EGKE (Einfache Gesellschaft Kunsthaus-Erweiterung / Ordinary Partnership Kunsthaus Extension), or to put it the other way around, the clients organised themselves as a body. No fundamental modifications to the concept were necessary. For urban-planning reasons, and due to political pressures, the block was set back from the square and the volume made 10 percent smaller. Some adjustments were also undertaken in the interior: the large stairway, for instance, was originally set diagonally to the hall but now runs lengthways.

Following page spread:

The large block of the third Kunsthaus closes Heimplatz and dominates it. Rank is not subjugation, commented the Building Appeals Court. The traffic is left out, both in the image and in the planning process. The intention was to plan a museum not a traffic solution.

75 Chipperfield 2009, p. 80.
76 Magazin 1/15, p. 34.

All of the gallery spaces in the second upper floor have skylighting, while most of those on the first floor have side lighting. Everywhere the exhibition spaces enjoy an impressive height of 4.80 metres – nowhere do the ceilings flatten our feelings. It goes without saying that the lighting, air-conditioning and security are all cutting-edge. The facade is covered with a perpendicular hatching of concrete ribs, which likewise cross the windows of the side-lit galleries and thus prevent rays of light from glancing off the glazing behind them. Moreover, they give the building a unified appearance, emphasising the block effect.

On 25 November 2012 the city's population agreed to the project, with around 54 percent voting 'yes' to it; in January 2013 the design plan came into effect; and on 31 May the city authorities issued building permission. As if out of nowhere, the Archicultura Foundation for Townscape and Landscape Care lodged a legal challenge against the decision, only for the Building Appeals Court to resolutely reject the complaint in December 2014 and charging them 35,000 francs in court fees and administrative charges, whereupon the foundation backed down. With the ruling the building permission became legally valid. The Kunstgesellschaft had originally planned to begin construction in 2013, which was halted by the appeals procedure, so that building was only able to commence in summer 2015. The planning interruption had cost a total of two million francs and caused two years of delays.

A lot has been written about the size of the new building, almost always accompanied by the opinion that it is too large. This is a twofold fallacy. On the one hand, in the century since the Moserbau, the Kunsthaus has risen from being a Zurich museum to an international one, as witnessed by the international plaudits for its temporary exhibitions. One only has to look at the other international institutions with which the Kunsthaus respectively cooperates in order to grasp which museum league the Kunsthaus plays in, namely the second. The new building is also a magnet for future donors, who would clearly like to see their bequests displayed. The Chipperfield Building is the Kunsthaus Zürich's architectural connection to the realities of the international museum world. On the other hand the new building embodies – just as the Moserbau did a hundred years before it – the status of the City of Zurich, this time in the year 2020. A new object of anxiety and magical

Facade section. The outer membrane of a museum mus perform a lot of functions. First it separates the outside from the inside. The windows are highly insulated. Then it m shield against the sun but allo the right amount of light to seep in, albeit not too much so as to dazzle. Security and safe are crucial factors. If a fire breaks out the ventilation flap should open automatically. All of this had to be resolved in an aesthetic manner fitting to exude the serenity of a majo art depository.

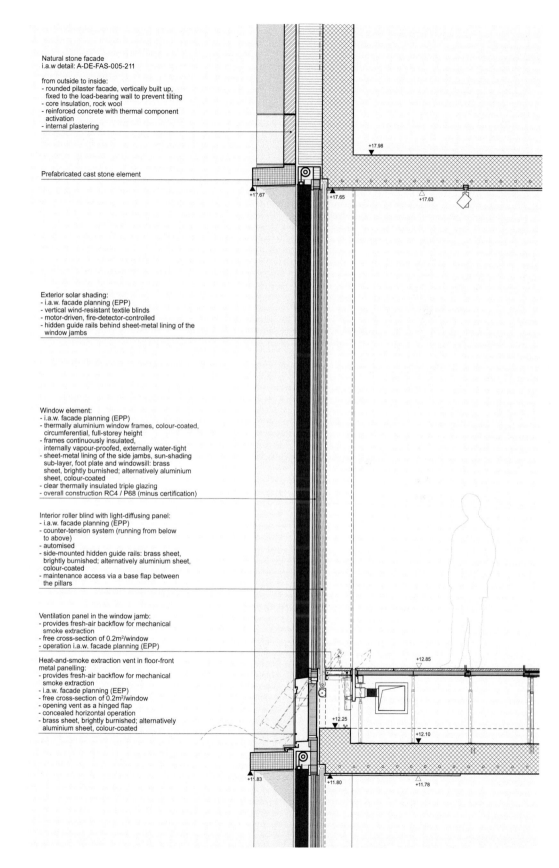

Natural stone facade
i.a.w detail: A-DE-FAS-005-211

from outside to inside:
- rounded pilaster facade, vertically built up,
  fixed to the load-bearing wall to prevent tilting
- core insulation, rock wool
- reinforced concrete with thermal component
  activation
- internal plastering

Prefabricated cast stone element

Exterior solar shading:
- i.a.w. facade planning (EPP)
- vertical wind-resistant textile blinds
- motor-driven, fire-detector-controlled
- hidden guide rails behind sheet-metal lining of the
  window jambs

Window element:
- i.a.w. facade planning (EPP)
- thermally aluminium window frames, colour-coated,
  circumferential, full-storey height
- frames continuously insulated,
  internally vapour-proofed, externally water-tight
- sheet-metal lining of the side jambs, sun-shading
  sub-layer, foot plate and windowsill: brass
  sheet, brightly burnished; alternatively aluminium
  sheet, colour-coated
- clear thermally insulated triple glazing
- overall construction RC4 / P68 (minus certification)

Interior roller blind with light-diffusing panel:
- i.a.w. facade planning (EPP)
- counter-tension system (running from below
  to above)
- automised
- side-mounted hidden guide rails: brass sheet,
  brightly burnished; alternatively aluminium sheet,
  colour-coated
- maintenance access via a base flap between
  the pillars

Ventilation panel in the window jamb:
- provides fresh-air backflow for mechanical
  smoke extraction
- free cross-section of 0.2m²/window
- operation i.a.w. facade planning (EPP)

Heat-and-smoke extraction vent in floor-front
metal panelling:
- provides fresh-air backflow for mechanical
  smoke extraction
- i.a.w. facade planning (EEP)
- free cross-section of 0.2m²/window
- opening vent as a hinged flap
- concealed horizontal operation
- brass sheet, brightly burnished; alternatively
  aluminium sheet, colour-coated

+17.98
+17.67
+17.65
+17.63
+12.85
+12.25
+12.10
+11.83
+11.80
+11.78

attraction has emerged – the fight for city rankings. When the city glances over its shoulder it no longer focuses on Basel and its valuable collections, but instead on Munich, Stuttgart, Lyons, Milan, with whom it vies for city tourists and purchasing-power flows.

Construction began on 3 August 2015 and the museum of the twenty-first century will open in phases during 2021.

The large hall is a public civic space. It breathes the spirit of a global city, the metropolis of Zurich in 2020. The stairway is set as a monumental ascent at the end of the hall, in keeping with Chipperfield's classicist stance.

# Layout Plans
# 1910–2020

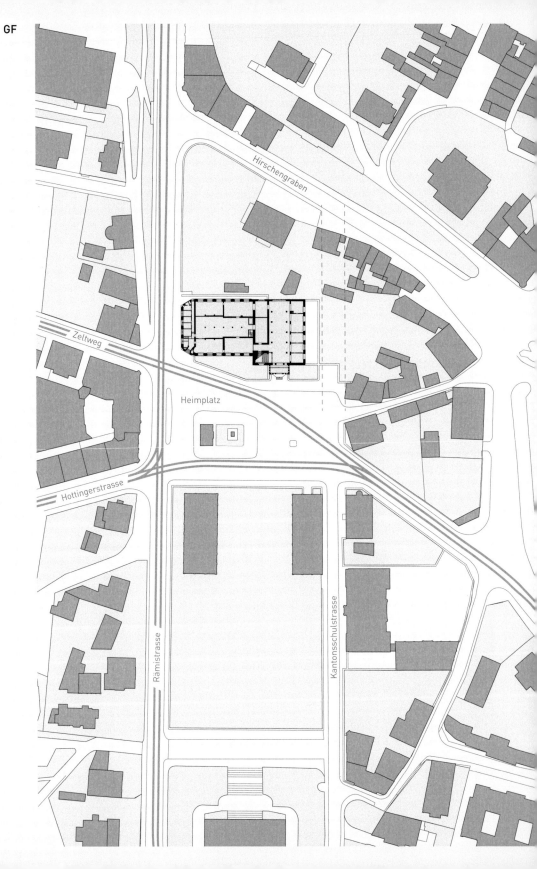

## 1ST FLOOR

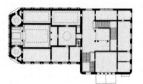

## 2ND FLOOR

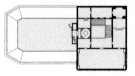

Site plan of the Kunsthaus as of 1910 with the positioned layouts of the ground floor plus the first and second floors. Facing the Old Town the old city structures are still preserved.

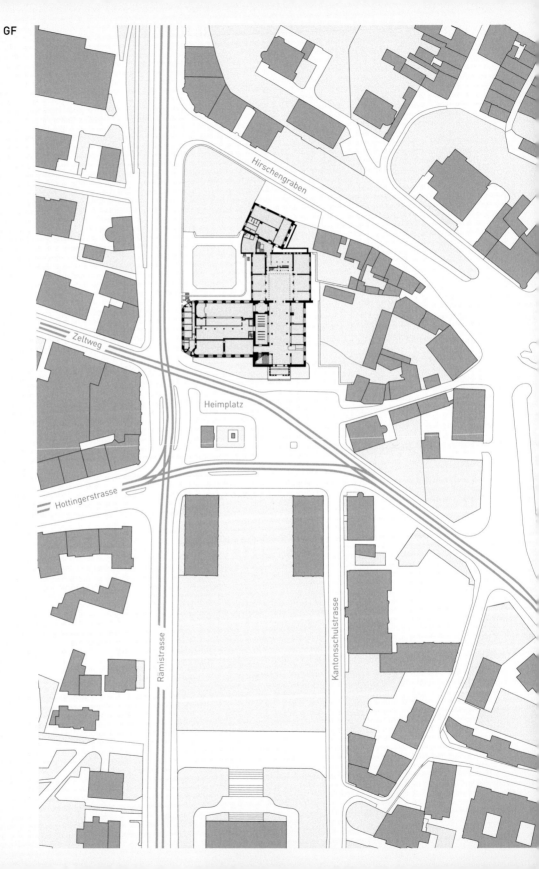

1925

GF

Hirschengraben

Zeltweg

Heimplatz

Hottingerstrasse

Rämistrasse

Kantonsschulstrasse

## 1ST FLOOR

## 2ND FLOOR

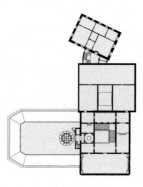

Site plan as of 1925 with the positioned layouts of the ground floor plus the first and second floors. The annexe closes the gap between the Collections Building and the Villa Landolt. The Kunsthaus is almost doubled in size.

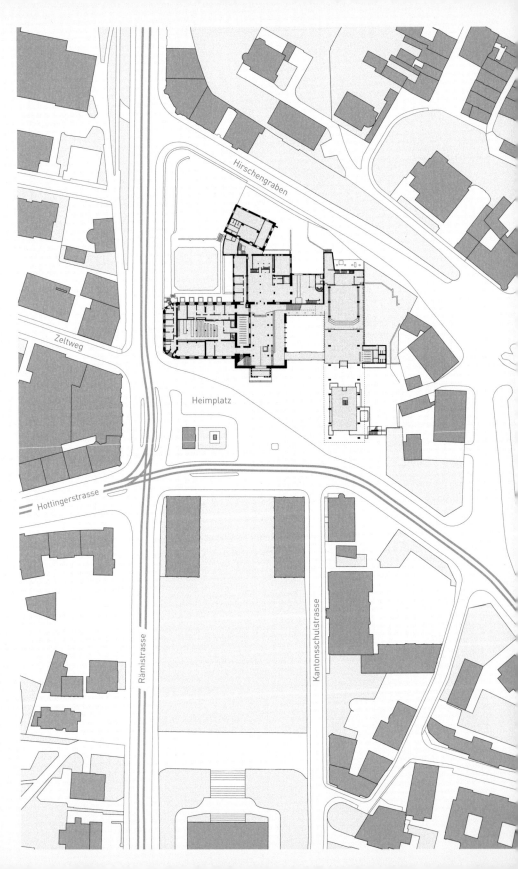

1959    GF

## 1ST FLOOR

## 2ND FLOOR

Site plan as of 1959 with positioned ground floor plus the first and second floors. The reading room is walled up; access to the Pfister Building is situated at the end of the original foyer. A garden courtyard lies between the new and the old building.

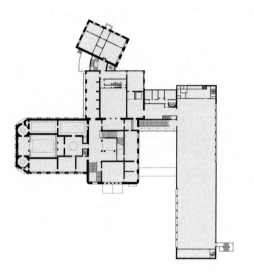

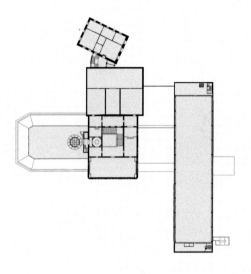

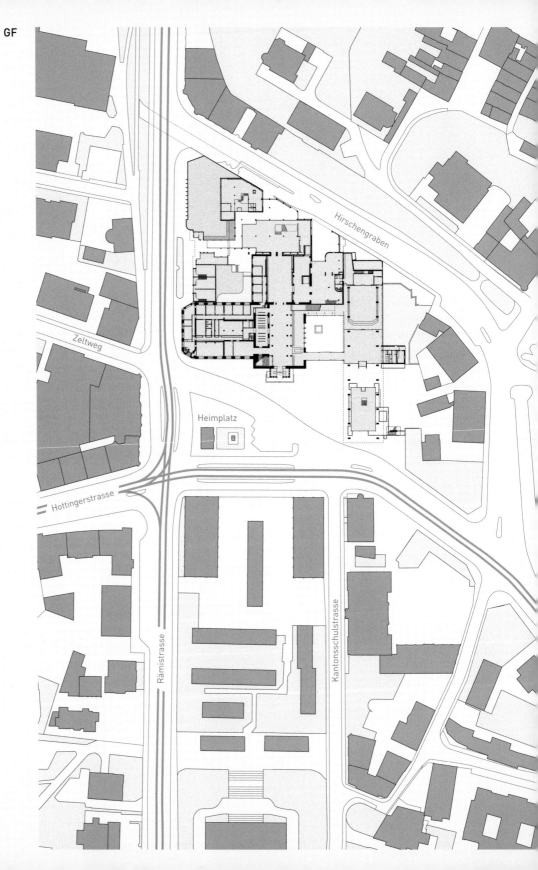

1976 GF

Hirschengraben

Zeltweg

Heimplatz

Hottingerstrasse

Rämistrasse

Kantonsschulstrasse

**1ST FLOOR**

**2ND FLOOR**

Site plan as of 1976 with positioned ground floor plus the first and second floors. The Villa Landolt has disappeared; the park of the Kantonsschule has been colonised with sheds.

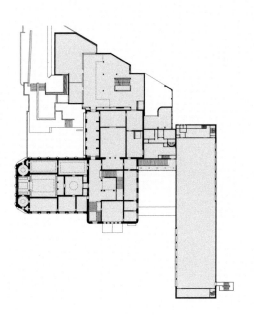

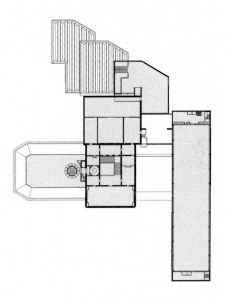

# 2020

GF

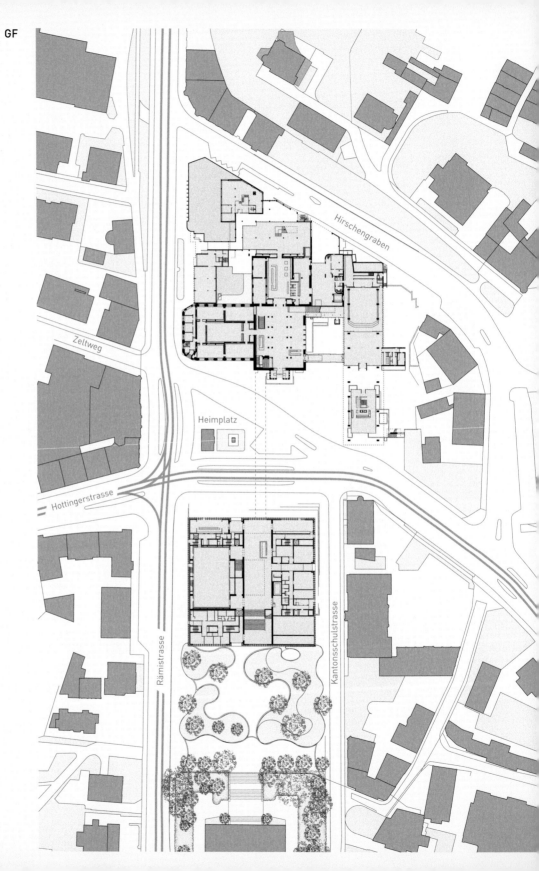

Hirschengraben

Zeltweg

Heimplatz

Hottingerstrasse

Rämistrasse

Kantonsschulstrasse

## 1ST FLOOR

## 2ND FLOOR

Site plan of the Kunsthaus as of 2020 with the positioned layouts of the ground floor plus the first and second floors. Heimplatz is enclosed; an art garden is created between the Chipperfield Building and the old Kantonsschule.

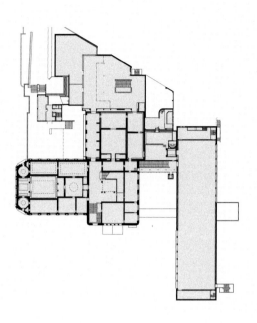

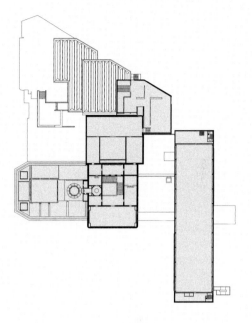

Layout Plans 1910–2020

Plan sources:
architects and various publications

Plan editing:
Werner Huber,
Łukasz Pietrzak

# BIBLIOGRAPHY

200 Jahre 1987: **200 Jahre Zürcher Kunstgesellschaft 1787–1987**, ed. Zürcher Kunstgesellschaft, Zurich 1987.

–

Bärtschi 1983: Hans-Peter Bärtschi: **Industrialisierung, Eisenbahnschlachten und Städtebau**, Basel/Boston/Stuttgart: Birkhäuser Verlag, 1983.

–

Bericht 1989: Bericht des Bauamtes II, 21. November 1989. (Jury report, study commission)

–

Buomberger 2015: Thomas Buomberger, 'Bührle als Kulturförderer: Eigennutz und Grosszügigkeit', in Thomas Buomberger and Guido Magnaguagno (eds.): **Schwarzbuch Bührle**, Zurich: Rotpunktverlag, 2015, pp. 159–80.

–

Chipperfield 2009: Interview with David Chipperfield by Sonja Lüthi, in **VISO** 01/2009.

–

City-Ring 1967: Stadtplanungsamt Zürich, **City-Ring: Bericht und Pläne**, Zurich, 1967.

–

Festschrift 1976: Zürcher Kunstgesellschaft (ed.), **Kunsthaus Zürich: Festschrift zur Eröffnung des Erweiterungsbaus 1976**, Zurich, 1976.

–

Geschichte Kt. ZH 1994: Bruno Fritzsche et al., **Geschichte des Kantons Zürich, vol. 3: 19. und 20. Jahrhundert**, Zurich: Werd Verlag, 1994.

–

Giedion 1922: Sigfried Giedion, **Spätbarocker und romantischer Klassizismus**, Munich: Bruckmann, 1922.

–

Hasche 2006: Katja Hasche, 'Neue Gebäudetechnik im Kunsthaus Zürich', in **tec 21** 35/2006, pp. 22–8.

–

Hochparterre Wettbewerbe: **Hochparterre Wettbewerbe**, 1/2009, Zurich 2009.

–

Jahresbericht 1946: **Jahresbericht**, ed. Zürcher Kunstgesellschaft, Zurich 1947.

–

Jahresbericht 1968: **Jahresbericht**, ed. Zürcher Kunstgesellschaft, Zurich 1969.

–

Jehle 1982: Ulrike Jehle-Schulte Strathaus, **Das Zürcher Kunsthaus: ein Museumsbau von Karl Moser**, Basel/Boston/Stuttgart: Birkhäuser Verlag, 1982.

–

Kunstmuseen 1995: Peter Bergmann et al.: **Schweizer Kunstmuseen. Bauten und Projekte 1980–1994** (exhib. cat. Kunsthaus Centre Pasquart, Biel), Biel: Architektur-Forum, 1995.

–

Linsmayer 2015: Charles Linsmayer, 'Blutgeld vom ersten bis zum letzten Rappen ...', in Thomas Buomberger and Guido Magnaguagno (eds.): **Schwarzbuch Bührle**, Zurich: Rotpunktverlag, 2015, pp. 129–48.

Lüpertz 1985: Markus Lüpertz, 'Kunst und Architektur', in **Neue Museumsbauten in der Bundesrepublik Deutschland** (exhib. cat. Deutsches Architekturmuseum, Frankfurt am Main), Stuttgart: Klett-Cotta, 1985, pp. 30–6.

–

Mack 1999: Gerhard Mack, **Kunstmuseen: Auf dem Weg ins 21. Jahrhundert**, Basel/Berlin/Boston: Birkhäuser Verlag, 1999.

–

Magazin: **Kunsthaus Zürich: Magazin, Mitteilungsblatt der Zürcher Kunstgesellschaft**, here 2015 and 2017, published four times a year.

–

Mitteilungen Kunstgesellschaft: **Mitteilungen der Zürcher Kunstgesellschaft**, ed. Zürcher Kunstgesellschaft, here 1991 and 2001.

–

Neubau Schauspielhaus 1964: 'Wettbewerb für einen Neubau des Schauspielhauses Zürich', Report by the Prize Jury, Bauamt II der Stadt Zürich, Zurich, 1964.

–

Neue Räume 2002: **Die neuen Räume: Alberto Giacometti im Kunsthaus Zürich**, ed. Zürcher Kunstgesellschaft, Zurich, 2002.

–

Neujahrsblatt 1911: **Neujahrsblatt der Zürcher Kunstgesellschaft 1911**, ed. Zürcher Kunstgesellschaft, Zurich, 1911, p. 44.

–

Rössling 1986: Wilfried Rössling, **Curjel & Moser Architekten in Karlsruhe**, Karlsruhe: Verlag C. F. Müller, 1986.

–

SBZ 77/19: **Schweizerische Bauzeitung**, 19, vol. 77, 7 May 1959.

–

Sondernummer 1995: **Kunsthaus Zürich: Magazin, Mitteilungsblatt der Zürcher Kunstgesellschaft**, special issue: 'Villa Tobler: Die schönste Jugendstilvilla Zürichs für das Kunsthaus', 4/1995.

–

Strebel 1990: Ernst Strebel, 'Umbauen, ergänzen, neu interpretieren' in **Werk, Bauen + Wohnen** 5/1990, pp. 14–18.

–

Studienauftrag 1989: 'Studienauftrag an mehrere Architekten zur Erlangung von Vorschlägen für eine räumliche Erweiterung des Kunsthauses', Bauamt II der Stadt Zürich, 9 February 1989.

–

Vonesch 1980: Gian-Willi Vonesch, **Der Architekt Gustav Albert Wegmann (1812–1858): ein Beitrag zur Zürcher Architekturgeschichte**, Zurich: Juris, 1980/81.

–

von Moos 2010: Stanislaus von Moos: 'Karl Moser. Die Kunst. Das Haus: Hand in Hand mit der Kunst seiner Zeit schafft Karl Moser ein modernes Museum', in **100 Jahre Kunsthaus Zürich**, NZZ special number, 17 April 2010, pp. 13–17.

# IMAGE CREDITS

**Page 9, top:** Baugeschichtliches Archiv Zürich, photograph Adolf Moser; **bottom:** Archiv ZKG/KHZ

**Page 12:** Baugeschichtliches Archiv Zürich, photograph Adolf Moser

**Page 17, top:** gta Archives/ETH Zurich, Karl Moser, photograph Ph. & E. Link; **bottom:** gta Archives/ETH Zurich, Karl Moser, photograph Ph. & E. Link

**Page 19, top:** gta Archives/ETH Zurich, Karl Moser; **bottom:** Archiv ZKG/KHZ

**Page 21:** gta Archives/ETH Zurich, Karl Moser

**Page 23, top:** gta Archives/ETH Zurich, Karl Moser; **bottom:** gta Archives/ETH Zurich, Karl Moser, photograph Heinrich Lunte

**Page 24, top:** Archiv ZKG/KHZ; **bottom:** Archiv ZKG/KHZ

**Page 26:** Archiv ZKG/KHZ

**Page 29:** gta Archives/ETH Zurich, Karl Moser

**Page 30:** gta Archives/ETH Zurich, Karl Moser

**Page 32:** Baugeschichtliches Archiv Zürich

**Page 35:** Schweizer Bauzeitung 77/19, p. 285

**Page 36:** Archiv ZKG/KHZ

**Page 37:** Photograph © Kai Konopacki

**Page 39:** City-Ring 1967, Beilage (supplement) 4

**Page 41:** Archiv ZKG/KHZ

**Page 44:** Archiv Walter Dräyer

**Page 45:** Archiv Walter Dräyer

**Page 47:** Werk, Bauen + Wohnen 5/1990, pp. 14–15

**Page 53:** Archive of plans, Kunsthaus Zürich

**Page 57:** Photograph Kunsthaus Zürich, Arthur Faust

**Page 62:** David Chipperfield Architects

**Page 65:** David Chipperfield Architects

**Page 66:** David Chipperfield Architects

## IMPRINT

This book is being published on the occasion of the opening of the Kunsthaus Zürich's new extension building in autumn of 2021.

Realised with funds from the Einfache Gesellschaft Kunsthaus-Erweiterung (EGKE).

–

Concept: Kunsthaus Zürich
Text: Benedikt Loderer
Translations into English: Thomas Skelton-Robinson
Proofreading: Colette Forder
Design: Büro4, Zürich
Plan editing: Werner Huber, Łukasz Pietrzak
Pre-press, printing and binding:
DZA Druckerei zu Altenburg GmbH, Thuringia

–

–

Verlag Scheidegger & Spiess
Niederdorfstrasse 54
8001 Zurich
Switzerland
www.scheidegger-spiess.ch

–

Scheidegger & Spiess is being supported by the Federal Office of Culture with a general subsidy for the years 2016–2020.

–

ISBN 978-3-85881-859-1

German edition:
ISBN 978-3-85881-676-4

French edition:
ISBN 978-3-85881-860-7